Introduction

I feel blessed to be introduced to real estate at the right time and by the right person. Right time, because I was not satisfied with what I was doing in my 'life' earlier. Right person, because who would not like to get introduced to the field by one of its legends. He had forewarned me about the unorganized playing field I was entering into and its list of surprises. May be he was checking my tenacity! Since then I have met and continue to meet many brokers, builders and players of this field, each one with their own ways of working, method, behaviour, understanding, logic and idiosyncrasies. They are so very indulged and embroiled into their working, issues and outcomes that they forget about the main character of this theatre on which they survive; the end-user. This short story is to make them aware of the role they play in this journey of the end-user who would leave the stage after their work is over but he has to remain on the stage to welcome the next hero of the play. It would be his character which would make the hero 'The Hero'. He forgets this important part of the field and ruins his image. This service sector industry is one of the best business schools in this part of the world. I would guarantee that any person succeeding in this (unfair) playing field can succeed in any other service fields.

This is not a preaching book, sermons or for that matter advise by some experienced or old professor but observations shared by young and inexperienced student with different prospective and dream in the form of a short stories. It is entirely up to the reader to contemplate about this long ignored real estate medium with new vintage point. I leave the decision to the reader whether they would like to just continue with the major lethargic attitude or get some fresh and effective direction in this long forgotten socially downgraded field to rise as 'phoenix'.

- Venky

Preface

"Any business, field or sector is driven by their consumer or end-users. Though she per se may be a small or tiny person but together they decide the drift of the market. The entire market is given direction by this end-user. End-user is very lazy and likes everything to be served on platter or rather spoon-fed. The multi billion dollar companies decide their strategies, marketing, financing, operations and other parameters of business on this single almost 'non existent' end user.

This end-user has lever of fate of these giants but sadly unaware of its ephemeral power".

Dedicated to realtors

This book is for people who need to know the field, who are real estate service providers or associated with it, who need to raise their status in society as professionals as well as remuneration. I agree completely with any person who says that the real estate is for earning money and not for charity.

I also firmly believe that the ultimate success of any business and profession is serving its customers and not oneself. When you serve customers and earn money, you serve the entire sector including yourself.

Acknowledgements

I acknowledge Mr. Murari Chaurvedi's influence; founder of Accommodation Times – a fortnightly newspaper for more than last three decades, who was the person responsible for my entry to real estate field. He is one of the stalwarts & legend in the field and his straight forward nature & moral values still guides me through the maze of crony capitalism prevalent in this sector. His legacy is carried forward by his two able sons Ajay & Sanjay.

I also acknowledge my wife Raani along with my daughters Nakshatra & Pavitra, being the pillar of strength and support system through out my entrepreneurial journey.

Journey of a Broker

Indian real estate stories

Part 1

Journey of a Broker

Part 2

Short Stories

Copyright@2018 Vinayak N Hanchate
All rights reserved
ISBN – 13: 978-1-9810-7902-5

Part 1 – **Journey of a Broker**

Chapter 1: Vishal Doshi	1
Chapter 2: A genuine broker	5
Chapter 3: Friends	16
Chapter 4: Soudda - The Deal	25
Chapter 5: Deal gone sour	37
Chapter 6: Mr. Ashok I. Lalka	45
Chapter 7: Boora Waqt …….Lessons	53
Chapter 8: Diksha	63
Chapter 9: Finance	73
Chapter 10: Investor	81
Chapter 11: To Boston...	91
Hindi words / dialects meaning	102

Part 2 – **Short Stories**

Short Story 1: Property Deal: Every Indian Story   **106**
Short Story 2: Wisdom in real estate investment   **113**
Short Story 3: Smile @ Architect   **115**
Short Story 4: Tale of Mumbi's Real Estate Investor   **120**
Short Story 5: Investment; the ultimate ecstasy   **127**
Short Story 6: Brokerage at stake!   **130**
Short Story 7: Black Pearl in the turbulent R E Ocean **135**
Short Story 8: Propety Brokers, Now your way!   **140**
Short Story 9: The Indian REALTOR   **148**

About the Author   **151**

Journey of a Broker

Chapter 1
Vishal Doshi

Vishal Doshi was in his late thirties and well-built for his age with a paunch getting obvious at places. He was missing Diksha, his wife who had gone to her parents' place which would be now a week's time. How he missed her during mornings......

A very peace loving character with hatred to violence, he was always calm though not the same in his teenage and younger times. He was famous for his tantrums in the society and lots of *'dadagiri'*.

But over a period, time had made him wiser earlier than necessary for his circumstances.

When he thought about his early days he smiled warmly...... He was a first class commerce graduate with no inclination to do a job or for that matter to work under anybody as was with all *gujarathis*. He started his *'dhanda'* as his fellow *'gujarathi'* and *'marwari'* friends did. He was into readymade garments because his father, Ramnikbhai Doshi was a garment shop owner and that was an obvious decision. But Vishal started his business during his father's last years of life when his father had suffered a huge loss in the shop.

He wanted to make it big in the ready-made garment sector. He used to do a lot of marketing and running around for his business. He was moderately successful and liked by most of garment traders because of his nature and friendly manner.

He did this stint for 4 years and then shifted to plastic packaging as he got bored with the garments. He tried this for next 3 years and was unsuccessful with it. The experience he gained for doing business was great but not so financially. His friends used to admire his conclusion of any situation. He had this earthy, approachable and 'easy to talk to' persona.

His stint with packaging business ended when he was sitting in his father's empty shop which was in the middle of market. He was thinking about the payment receivables from 4-5 customers and frankly was doubtful about it for at least 6 months. He did not have any money with him except for few thousands in the bank to sustain his daily consumption. His mother was keeping ill for a long time after his father's death.

When he was sitting in his shop, Panchalbhai from neighbourhood shops said,

'Aare Vishalbhai, aapke paas itne jaga hai thoda mujhe jaga de do mere tailoring shopke liye'.

'Kitna bhaada doge Panchalbhai?'

'Jo market ka rate hai woh lelijiye' said Panchal.

'Aap side ki jagah hai na woh lelijiye. Uska darwaza bhi alag hai. Chalegaa?' Vishal asked. 'Aare woh to badiya rahega

mere liye, bus mera board lagane dijiye aage ke taraf '
Panchalbhai said.

'Theekhai aap aadhe jagah par board laga lijiye. Deposit kitna doge aap?'

'Aare jo deposit aabhi jeen ke paas hai woh aap lelijiye' said Panchal.

'Kabhi aiange aap?' asked Vishal

'Aap bole to kal aa jaunga…..

'Theek hai aajaeeye….

'Toh yeh lejiye token ke paisee….

'Aare Panchalbhai, hum aapko kitne saalose jaante hai, aap hi meri pant banate hoh, aapse kya token lu'.

Panchalbhai said, *'Vishalbhai vyawahar to vwawahar hai, usme kyo guunjaaish nahi. Aapke pitaji ki sikh hai aur mujhe hamesha kaam aati hai. Mein bhi doosare ke saat vyawahar ekdam chokha rakta hu'.*

'Theek hai, theek hai…..

Vishal thought thanks to my father, I have now an asset which would give me a constant income.

He even started respecting his father's long vision.

In a week's time Panchalbhai had settled and there were occasional queries for his front sided section of his shop.

Vishal thought there is a lot of demand for property in this market. Why not start an estate agency?

So he enquired with some neighbouring brokers to know about the scope of this sector. He got a mixed response, but decided to go ahead because of his shop in the main market region. He got a banner made named "Vishal Estate Agency". Within six months, he did two small deals. Meanwhile, he received his pending amount from the previous business. He was feeling better and also gave encouraging response to his mother's insistence about his marriage.

In the next four months he got married to Diksha.

Diksha was one of the three daughters from a middle class background and a college dropout.

She was fairly good-looking and suitable for Vishal in lot of many aspects.

While she was bubbly and chirpy, Vishal was calm and balanced. She could talk endlessly while Vishal could listen endlessly. But within a year's time of his marriage his mother expired and Vishal drew close to and dependant on Diksha.

Vishal used to hate socializing and moving around while Diksha used to pull him from the shop to visit different places like their relatives and shopping.

Over a period of time, Diksha gave up on Vishal and left him to his shop and business. But, Vishal never stopped Diksha from doing whatever she enjoyed; only he insisted on her food which was delicious and having morning cup of tea with her. She looked very beautiful during the morning tea session just after her bath.

So they had settled and were blessed with a son; now two years old.

How badly he was missing her……

Journey of a Broker

Chapter 2
A genuine broker

Vishal, a real estate agent had realized early that this field does not have respect like any other field. This was one of the least interested and 'liked' field by educated people. When *'dalal'* or broker is uttered an image is created in any average person's mind of an obese individual chewing *'paan'* with lot of gold ornaments all over his body or if any concession given then, a lean hyperactive and talkative person with no commitment or loyalty. Everybody thought anyone can be a broker as no license or degree was needed. Hence the market was full of unethical, unprofessional and any *'Nathu Khaira'* (Tom, Dick or Harry of western world) broker. Vishal knew this was true but not the complete picture. Real estate has changed a lot but the public psyche of a broker has not evaded completely. The broker is the first liability for any seller or buyer. He also knew if tapped properly this is the most enriching field and most unexplored field professionally. He had a vague idea of professionalism of brokers in western world. He had this strong inclination of getting professionalism in this field. He knew majority or at least fifty percent brokers came for easy money in this field and after realizing the grind and sector change their field or continue it as a 'side' business. Many brokers did not understand about the field itself and its nuances as no professional guidance was present predominantly in market. The sector was going through a slow process of professionalism as people were asking or rather demanding from the field. With invent of digital technology it was at its exponential growth trajectory. The market was struggling to incorporate the technology in the field with lots of failures and few successes. It would achieve its full growth in the coming years. Vishal attended many related seminars or workshops to understand the field. He was reading lot of information about the field whenever or wherever possible. He had the urge to get some professionalism and regulation into the field. He had discussed these things with some seasoned brokers but with absolutely no or any encouraging responses. Sometimes he thought the players of this field were their own enemies. They did not realize that by leaving their comfort zone they would have tremendous successful potential. But they were happy with what they had and did not intend to disturb their peaceful 'applecart'.

Vishal was once witness to one discussion…. no it was an argument between two senior brokers over the valuation of the property. Vishal had visited the brokers with some other colleague for some deal. The discussion had come to where the accompanied colleague, Chetanbhai asked one of the senior brokers about the price of the property. He wanted to know the price so that he could convey the approximate budget to the customer so that they in turn would arrange for corresponding loan amount. One of the senior brokers, Ojasbhai, was saying, ask the customers their budget and then quote the price, ofcourse within the price range. But other senior broker, Jigneshbhai, was saying to quote the lowest to median price of that locality, basically favouring the buyer.

Then Vishal had asked a very important question unknowingly, *'who and how do you decide the price? What is the correct valuation method?*

Ojasbhai said, *'Seller decides the value of the property.'*

Jigneshbhai retorted by saying *'no… buyer should decide the price.'*

'In that case let the markets decide the price' said Ojasbhai.

'Market is made up of brokers like us and we do not follow the dictum of the buyer' said Jigneshbhai.

"*Buyer has come to the market to buy and he will take or leave the product if affordable to him and not decide the price of the product.'*

'In this way no market will ever remain stable and you would have lot of punters and opportunistic people.'

'That is the reason, let market decide the price' said Ojasbhai.

'Market is always dynamic, more so in earlier stages but as it becomes matured the market stabilizes. But at this stage too some of them try to dictate the market and try getting more and more profit out of the buyers. For some more

commission they lured the sellers for more price. That is the reason the seller turns greedy and wants the maximum selling price. For that he goes to so many brokers and almost everyone raises the price of the property inflating the market. That is not the right price.'

Ojasbhai was getting little excited. He said, *'Jigneshbhai, let us assume one family needs a property in western suburbs and the head or the main earning person of the family had to go townside for work. He will like to stay in a place nearer to work place but because of his budget he decides on the nearest suburb. Now he enquires about the price of the locality and after looking out for his need he decides on the property. He has to offer the price to the seller but the seller says 'no' as he would get more price in the market. So now why should the seller agree to buyer's price and take the loss Jigneshbhai?'*

Jigneshbhai said coolly, *'because the buyer may also get a seller with lesser price as the seller may get higher from someone else. Depending on the urgency the seller decides to give away the property and depending upon the necessity the buyer would take the property. The buyer could wait for some more time but the seller may not wait. So the buyer decides the price.'*

'The situation could also be reversed' said Ojasbhai.

'In that case the number of deals would decide the market and not individual deal. Because one of the parameters of

travelling for buyer as you mentioned forms the important one. But you also have a situation where the buyer need not have to travel so much and for him the traveling may not form the criteria for his purchase.'

'You could then safely assume that the number of people buying with this criteria is less than the family where traveling is important; that is businessman or self-employed having a shop or office nearby as against employee. For every one businessman or self-employed there are at least 5-6 employees', said Ojasbhai.

'But the businessman would get a better property than existing one and may buy it at same rate somewhere else so why should he buy it here. Also the employee would like to lower the price as much as possible.'

The discussion was going on and on but Vishal had a question to both of them.

He asked, *'the buyer is a seller in future and the seller has been a buyer in the past, so how one does decides whom the market is favouring?'*

The discussion had continued and continued and both the brokers were still arguing when Vishal had left them.

Once when he was about to leave his office for lunch, he received one couple struggling from the afternoon heat to his place. He made them comfortable with cold water and sugarcane juice from nearby shop. They were very happy with this small gesture and started pouring out all their problems in getting the right property. Their main complaint was, not a single broker had a property matching their need and requirement. The brokers were trying to sell what they had with them without considering or overlooking the couples' need. This was a common phenomenon with the brokers; some did it rudely by saying this kind of property is not available anywhere in the market or by sweet talking the customers. Very few wanted to take effort for the customers or did not have the property needed.

Vishal was well aware of this but because brokers had to survive they use different methods to make a deal. He asked them their need and filled in the form which he had made with great effort and inputs over a period of time. The couple was impressed by this kind of approach. As they were educated they liked this approach. Vishal asked them their need and trying to get their goal on paper. This took about half an hour with most talking done by the wife, Vidya and revealing their innermost desire for house. At the end of the discussion Vishal had asked them some questions leading to specifics and some refinement in their goals. They themselves were very clear of the requirement to large extent now. Vishal knew the property is not available or rather not easily available in the market and he would need time and commitment from the customers. But there was a problem with the deal as with all the deals, about the customer's loyalty to brokers. So he was careful in asking them about it.

Journey of a Broker

He said 'I need to search the market for the availability but it would need time and little patience from you.'
The man; Sushant understood and said 'Vishalbhai if you give us assurance of the right property then we will not be going to any other broker. And with you, we both are comfortable hence we like to stick with you for some time.'
Vishal said 'thank you, but you have to wait for at least two months duration to get the property.' 'Of course, we understand that and with you we would hold on for two months (after getting a nod from his wife).'
After their departure and more information about whom they went to he was in deep thought. He was thinking about this opportunity of giving professional services to the couple. He was slowly forming a plan for it when the shrill of telephone ring brought him to the present reality. It was his wife Diksha waiting at home for lunch. His helper an elderly person, whom everybody called '*Kaka*', was relieved because he would now get to eat his lunch. After usual instructions to *Kaka*,

Vishal left his place to go to his house nearby but without much eagerness as every day. He was in his thought till the food was served to him. The aroma brought him to his normal senses and the food had replaced the customer in few seconds. He was all praise for his wife's culinary skill and blamed her for his paunch.

After their usual afternoon break of about one hour he was back at his shop. He was still thinking about the customers when the telephone rang. Vishal picked up the receiver to answer Maheshbhai, a nearby broker.

Maheshbhai said, '*Vishalbhai kaiso ho? Dhandha paani theekh thak?*'

Vishalbhai knew Maheshbhai to be a shrewd person and fully aware of the reason of the phone call.

He responded by saying, '*Hha hha Maheshbhai, mein theek hu. Aap kaise ho?*

The couple had mentioned Vishal about few brokers they had visited and Maheshbhai was one of them.

He responded after listening to Maheshbhai, '*Maheshbhai, woh family mere paas bhi aaye thee. Meinbhi unke liye dhund raha hui. Aap hi mujhe batana agar kuch aachi aur unke layak property nikalti hai to.*'

The line was silent for some time. Vishal was smiling to himself and knowing Maheshbhai must be thinking where else had the customer been to? More brokers they go to, more is the competition between the brokers. As expected, Maheshbhai put an end to the conversation earnestly with hollow sounding good bye.

Vishal knew this to be the problem with lot of customers but the fault lied with both, the brokers and customers but more so with brokers. They being greedy would like to go to any extent to woo the customers. You need to stop this *'khichdi'* in the market. He was aware that the bigger and reputed consultant signs a contract with the customer before starting the work. But these customers usually were high profile and corporate or qualified people. They hate dealing with unprofessional brokers.

This small time problem with middle class locality like his was solved by having a direct proposal from the seller. This was not always the case as the sellers used to go to lot of brokers in the vicinity as they wanted to dispose of the property faster and with competitive rates. Each broker gave the seller higher hope for the price and thus the market got inflated. There was greediness all around. Some of them said it is business and supply demand game. More you ask more you get.

As customers were not going to reduce in near future especially in matured market like his the price never comes down. The price may remain stable for some time but rarely goes down in real estate, that too in Mumbai. He was having a vague idea of a business model in his mind which would tackle this issue to some extent. He needed lot of thinking and refining of the model with lot of inputs and discussion with evolved personnel from the field.

As far as the present issue was concerned he knew what he had to do. He got all his data and shortlisted all the desirable properties but knew very few or none would be matching with the customer's need. He now went through all the societies and buildings in the vicinity (he had kept the data which was updated) and short-listed the matching ones. He properly put everything on paper and called Kaka. He gave instructions to *Kaka* with his visiting cards. *Kaka* was supposed to go to all the short-listed buildings and meet the society security or manager. He was supposed to give the card to them and call from his mobile to Vishal. He would talk to the concerned person (or perhaps secretary and chairman of the society) and ask for the availability of the flats. He almost knew all the buildings and society people as he was a localite and was residing in this area since birth. So contact with them was not an issue but knowing the availability was. He had to be in touch with them persistently. He had instructed *Kaka* to have good relationship with the security guards as they were sometimes the real informer. Security guards used to have chai with *Kaka* at his shop and he used to encourage it to some extent.

After almost 3-4 weeks he had about four to five properties with him matching eighty percent of the customer's needs. He used to inform or remain in touch with the customer during weekends. In the fourth week he had asked them to visit the property. They were happy with the choice but not completely. He ask them for some more time and within next two weeks he was able to show them almost four more desirable properties. Sushant and Vidya, the couple were happy with the later choice of flats and short-listed two of them.

The deal was done in next week and the formalities completed within one and half months. Vishal was invited to their 'house-warming' ceremony. He was introduced to many of their friends and relative and was officially announced as their property consultant.

Sushant was telling his friend, *'Vishalbhai here really took lot of efforts to search our place. He really guided us through the entire procedure. Without him it was difficult to find the right kind of property. He had a very professional approach. He is a true property consultant.'*

Vidya agreed and said, *'Vishalbhai is a truly a genuine broker. For any advice on property we will approach him first.'*

Chapter 3
Friends

Vishal was sitting in pensive mood contemplating about the property in his locality which was not more than 1 kilometre form his shop. He knew the locality very well as he was born and brought up in Borivali east with schooling in nearby JB school. His concern right now was whether his investor; his long-time friend, an NRI would get good returns. This friend named Rajeev wanted to invest in their locality where he had small 1 RK flat (1 room kitchen) which was not occupied as he had lost his parents and used it when he came to India. He was interested in investing in this new finished project which had come up 3-4 months earlier by a local reputed builder. Vishal knew the builder not closely but professionally. The builder had a good track record of projects in the nearby locality. This was his major big project in Borivali east region. Vishal knew the builder via Asifbhai who was from the builder's locality at Goregaon. He thought of going for the deal after consulting Asifbhai. The project was good and near to Western Express highway and station connecting to western state of Gujarat. The project had good chances of appreciation in future. There were old buildings about more than 40 years age in this locality and would undergo re-development sooner or later. So the location and market stage was good. He wanted to be sure because it was one of his friend's investments and he did not want to take any chances. He knew Rajeev as *'chaddi buddy'* and Rajeev never showed any arrogance or high handedness when he interacted with Vishal. They were not very good friends but their fathers were very good friends. Rajeev's father used to work in the bank as an accountant. Vishal's father was indebted to Rajeev's father because he had helped him in some major bank accounting goof up. Rajeev's father had helped Vishal's father in sorting out the problem judiciously for nearly 6 months. In fact the bank manager had appreciated and applauded him in front of his staff. Rajeev's father was responsible for Vishal's graduation too. Vishal's father, Ramnikbhai, had taken him to Rajeev's father first after hearing of his son's graduated in first class. Rajeev had graduated with distinction in science and was pursuing his Phd after receiving scholarship and invitation from distinguished college at Boston, USA. He was now working with world renowned pharmaceutical company and risen to assistant director of R&D department. He had settled in USA with similar professional wife and a daughter. He had kept the place at Mumbai for sentimental reason and had all his relatives in Pune. He had money to invest and thought of investing in Mumbai as the returns would be good and if at all he thought of migrating back to India.

      Vishal and Asifbhai were good friends since last 3 years along with Manoj Gawde and Ashok Lalka due to one big deal. The money for that deal had not come to them yet. This friendship had come about gradually and with some hesitation as all four had nothing in common.

The story goes like this....

It was raining heavily about 3 years back and Manoj Gawde had got Asifbhai to Vishal's shop along with another broker Gattubhai. Gattubhai was a local broker and had a *'kholi'* in nearby Goregaon region. Gattubhai knew Manoj as he belonged to the same society of chawls. It was about more than 60 years old, had about 160 tenants residing in it and BMC had declared it in dilapidated condition. Gattubhai was a small local broker who had come across Shirishbhai, a bigger broker during the society meetings. After the knowledge of Gathubhai's line of activity, Shirishbhai entrusted him to look for builder/developers. Gattu had informed Manoj about it. Both were school dropouts who had settled for small time property brokerage activity after lot of failed attempts in other so called *'buzyness'*. Gattu was a good talker and worker but had one weakness. He was drunkard and every day after 8 pm he would be at the local bar with his quota of *'mausambi'* or *'narangi'*. Manoj was the hard working type and sincere but absolutely no business sense. Hence both of them tried lots of things, though separately but could not be successful in any of their ventures.

Journey of a Broker

After knowing the proposals from Shirishbhai, Manoj knew one good broker or rather heard about Vishal through *kaka*; his neighbour at the *kholi*. *Kaka* used to work with Vishal since a long time and had mentioned him to Manoj. In fact Manoj had met Vishal once or twice at his shop. So the proposal was brought to Vishal. Vishal heard the proposal but was not sure of the details as he knew the small time broker never got the details right. But at the same time he never revoked or insulted them because if treated properly they were great source of information to him.

'*Manoj...kaun aapke chawl ko kharidna chahata hai?*'

Manoj said, '*Kharidna nahi, bechana chahata hein...hum sab log jo waha rahete hai woh...*'

Vishal asked '*Toh kaun bechaney me madat kar raha hai?*'

'*Shirishbhai jo bahut bade dalaal hai...inka bada office hai Andheri mein*' Gattu said.

'*Kyo bechana chata hai?*' Vishal asked softly

'*Aare sab ghar tutne ko aaya hai na...muncipalitywala bola na*'. Gattu spurted out.

'*Kitne log rahte hai waha?*'

'*Sab mila ke 4 building hai aur ek maley pe 10 kholi. Kaka bhi udhar hi rahete hai*'. Manoj said '*Aur kitne maaley hai*'.

'*Ground aur 3 maaley*' said Gattu.

When Vishal heard the half baked proposal he instantly knew it was a big deal if done. He thought of giving it a try because it had come from the person staying in the same *chawl* and information would be easily accessible. He thought about people whom he should contact. He knew no builder/developer directly. So he contacted one acquaintance in Borivali west region. That person gave him the contact of Asifbhai who knew some builders. He told Gattu and Manoj to come next day.

Vishal as far as possible never roamed about much unless very important, but that was compensated by his listening skills. He was in fact very good at listening, so much so that he had not uttered a complete sentence during a deal which lasted for 2 hours. He was good at assessing the person and with his listening skills; he could exactly join the dots and nail the deal. His drawback was he used to do comparatively small deals which he became aware of later, in the coming years. His opinion counted in his circle of brokers. Everybody respected his opinion and when his soft voice spoke everyone heard. He could get clarity of the situation and analyze the problem with a win-win solution. He was respected not because he was commerce graduate but more because he would come with solutions benefiting all the parties concerned.

Next day he contacted Asifbhai and told him to meet him at his shop. Asifbhai said he has never visited Borivali east as he stays at Goregaon. Brokers have this unsaid code in common, "Not to spend a penny till the deal is genuine".

Vishal knew this, so told Asifbhai to give him his address at Goregaon and told he would send Manoj to fetch him.

So it was on a heavy rainy day that Manoj and Asifbhai had come to his shop along with Gattu. Meanwhile Vishal had got all the information about the proposal from Shirishbhai whose contact he had got through Gattu. Asifbhai was an elderly person with typical Muslim beard and moustache which had turned grey for his fifty two plus age with gentle mannerism. He knew *hindi, gujarati* and *marathi* languages well, because his ancestor had inhabited Mumbai with lot of other families from Gujarat.

Asifbhai gave a warm smile and said, *'Salam Vishalbhai...'*

Vishal said, *'Salam Asifbhai, please bethiye aap'*.

Vishal's thought process had begun to spur, like a machine when turned on.

He addressed me by my name and has warm smile meaning a confident and mannered person.

'Kya piyege aap? Chai. Coffe ya kuch thanda?' Vishal asked

'Chai chalegi...'

'Kaka, jara sab ke leye special chai bolna'.

Asifbhai looked at Vishal far more longer time than necessary and then looked around the shop.

'Pehle koi doosra dhanda karte thay kya aap?' Vishal thought he is assessing me now.

'Ha pehle mere pitaji readymade garments ki dukaan chalate thay..Meine usko aage nahi badhaya'.

'Aachha, iske liye bahut saare kaanch ke kapat hai. Aapki jagah market mein mauke ki jagah per hai....aapka dhanda to chalta rahega...kyu band kar diya aapne?'

Good inference and way of asking about my present status, Vishal thought.

Before replying he thought for a flash of a second whether to tell him the truth or not, but his instinct said Asifbhai was a good person and asking for right reason.

He said, 'mere pitaji ko kuch saal pehle jab me pad raha tha tab bahut nuksan ho gaya. Phir woh wapas dhanda karne nahi aaye dukan me. Dukan bahot saal tak khali padi rahi. Ab woh duniya me nahi rahe. Mein jab property ka kam karne laga tab ye dukaan meine phirse istmaal karna shuru kiya. Yeh kaka mere pitaji ke saat yaha kaam karte they'.

'Ha ha, bohut dev manoos Ramnikbhai...uska ladka bhi bilkul uske jaisa hai. Isle mein yaha kam karta hu'. Kaka said placing the tea glass on the table near Asifbhai.

Asifbhai said, 'aachha aachha, bahut aachha.... Aapke pitaji ke bareme sunke bura laga'.

Vishal thought now starts the waiting game....there was a long pause of touching the tea glass, lifting it, smiling and sipping the tea.

No response from Asifbhai yet. Vishal knew he had to be quiet for some time and answer only after he was asked. This would decide the fate of the meeting.

'Chai aachi hai...'Asifbhai uttered.

Journey of a Broker

Long pause again. Vishal was good at waiting game; he can remain speechless for hours together. He had cultivated this skill from his mother who was a very mild manner lady but strong a support to his father. He had understood the power of remaining quite. With patience the person in front would reveal everything. But he knew Asifbhai was not the one to reveal. His beard had not turned grey without reason.

There was some restlessness among Gattu and Manoj. Gattu said they needed to go out for some urgent matter. Vishal knew that the urgent matter was smoking cigarettes. Vishal had instructed both of them to be quite during the meeting.

Now it was only Vishal and Asifbhai.

Vishal gave a smile and sat still looking warmly at Asifbhai sipping his tea.

At last Asifbhai said: *'Gattubhai and Manojbhai ne bataya ke aapke pas koi redevelopment ka proposal hai'.*

So he blinked first....thought Vishal.

He was now ready to give the proposal. He had gathered the information from Shirishbhai and formulated into a proper format to present to builder. He explained the details of proposal but soon realized that Asifbhai was not interested in the technical aspects. He just asked who the members were and since how long they were staying there. What are their expectations compared to the market rate. He was very specific about the landowner and wanted to know all the details. Vishal called Manoj and Gattu inside and told them to answer all Asifbhai's question of the landowner. The meeting took about less than 45 minutes. At last Asifbhai said he had some three builders with him but needed to ask them about the proposals and would convey the result in a week's time. Vishal said, *'theek hai Asifbhai.aap bata dijiye hafte bharme'*. Asifbhai said warmly while leaving, *'Aacha laga aapko mil ke…'*

Vishal could say yes because it was seen in Asifbhai's eyes.

Chapter 4
Soudda - The Deal

A week passed by with intermittent visits from Manoj and Gattu. After a week's time only Manoj was seen visiting. Vishal knew the Gattu type; they would not last for long time. They are short time sprinklers. Real estate is a patient game and need lots of restraint.

He knew he should not call Asifbhai because that would show desperation and hence less money. He thought if Asifbhai had ready builders with him then he will contact him but if not then he would delay it till he finds an alternative. If it is beyond his capacity then Asifbhai would not call at all.

Vishal thought to wait for 2 weeks.

The call came after 10 days.

Asifbhai said, *'Salam Vishalbhai'*

'Salam Asifbhai', replied Vishal.

'Meine mere builder dosto se baat kiya hai lekein kisi ke pas samay nahi hai.....'

Vishal thought he is lying.

'Toh mein ye soch raha hu ki aap mere builder ke office mein aajaaiaye, toh unhe samajane mein aasani hogi' Asifbhai said

Vishal thought that means he wants time but likes the deal.

'Aacha Asifbhai, aap bataeye kabhi aur kaha aana hai'.

'Mein aapko phirse phone karunga'.

'*Theek hai*', said Vishal before replacing the receiver.
Vishal started thinking furiously about the situation. He thought if Asifbhai has liked the deal then why is he not forwarding it to the builders? Either he does not have them or there is some other problem. He, not having the builder was ruled out as his reference was given by a known reputed broker of the western region. So there has to be another issue and needs more time. That means he is trying another builder outside his circle. Should Vishal try for other brokers to search for other builders? He thought against it. He thought 'let me wait'.

Few days later Asifbhai called up and said he needs another meeting with him.

Vishal was waiting for him at his shop since 4 pm and this time he had not informed Manoj about it as he was not sure about what would happen. So better to keep him away for the time being.

Asifbhai came along with one elderly person who was of the same age.

He introduced him as Mr. Ashok Lalka form Borivali west. Vishal had heard vaguely about him but never met him.

Asifbhai said after the tea was placed before all of them,

'*VIshalbhai yeh Ashokbhai bohut saare builders ko janatey hai...*'

So one more broker involved, Vishal thought. Asifbhai understood want Vishal was thinking.

He said, *'Vishalbhai aapko sach bolta hu, mere saare builders ne bahut saara kaam haat me leya hai aur woh iitna bada kaam nahi kar paaege. Ek ne to aapke nazdik hi project chalu kiya hai.*

Yehi koi aada ek kilometer ki doori per hai'.

(This was the same project Vishal NRI friend Rajeev was interested later).

Vishal thought so that is the issue.

Ashokbhai was listening and looking around the place.

Vishal said *'koi baat nahi Asifbhai hum sab saat me kaam karege'.*

Asifbhai gave him a smile and look towards Ashokbhai. Ashokbhai was about 54 to 55 years old with good dressing sense and would appear as some administrator in some semi-government office. He had the habit of talking in point wise and very straightforward manner almost to the point of sounding rude. He sounded very greedy money wise but had good technical knowledge. He was an old college dropout. He also did lot of registration and stamp duty work of property. He was very good in technical details of property. So he started asking Vishal about the proposal. Asifbhai was looking out of place and just listening to their conversation. After understanding the details Ashokbhai said, *'dekho Vishalji I do have 1-2 builders who may be interested in it. You need to give me the copies of documents. If you want you could accompany me to them'.*

Vishal said, *'Aare nahi Ashokbhai, aapko Asifbhai leke aaye hai to aap pe pura vishwas hai ki aap ye documents market me ghoomaaige nahi'.*

Ashokbhai asked, *'Aur kitne log hey iss deal mein?'*

Vishal said, *'Shirishbhai, Gattu, Manoj, Mein, Asifbhai aur aap'.*

So there were 6 people involved. There was a long pause, enough to calculate the division of money involved. The project was about not less than100 crores and each would get big amount from it. In fact Ashokbhai was the only person who was exposed to such deals but had been successful only once that too as one of the 10th person. He was not so much interested in this kind of deals if it comes via so many people. It takes long time to break such kind of deal. He knew there would be lot of complication within the group of brokers are involved.

He told both of them that before approaching any builder he should call all the brokers involved and get the matter cleared before any misunderstanding happened. All three agreed and decided to meet in 2-3 days' time at Vishal's shop.

After 3 days, at 5pm all started trickling in. First to come was Manoj, then Asifbhai and Ashokbhai together. Last to arrive was Shirishbhai. Vishal asked Manoj about Gattu.

Monaj said, *'Woh to nahi aayega, kyoki woh Bambai chod ke chala gaya hai apne gaaon. Woh bahut pine laga tha aur* uski biwi bechari perashaan hoke uske maa baap ko bula liya. Woh unhe leker chale gaye'.

'Vapas aajayge to....' Ashokbhai asked.

'Nahi aayege Ashokbhai...Shirishbhai ko puchho....' Shirishbhai said, 'Uske pitaji aur maa aaye the mere pass aur unhone kaha ki jab bhi woh kholi bechana hoga to unhe gaon se bula le, tabhi woh Gattu aur uski missus ko leke aajayege aur sign kardege'.

'Uske pass paise nahi denoko bole kyoki woh peene me uda denga, uski aaurat bollii....' Manoj said.

'Ha.. uske paise fixed deposit me dalnoko bola hai' Shirishbhai completed.

So Gattu was out of picture, thought Vishal and everyone else also thought the same.

'Toh ab paanch log hai.....' Asifbhai said.

Shirishbhai said, 'Mein mere tarike se bhi doosere builder ko try kar raha hu.... Jo pehle ho jaayega aur aachha deal karega woh hum karenge. Aap sab ko manjoor haii? Lekin jo doosera deal hoga usme aap log nahi rahege'. Vishal thought now comes the tense moment.

'Doosarre builder aapke ke kuan hai?' Ashokbhai asked

'Hai mere poorane pechan ke, Sab Bandra aur us taraf se hai. Aap ke kaun builder hai Ashokbhai', Shirishbhai asked.

'Mere ek Borivali aur Malad se hai aur ek Santacruz se hai' Ashokbhai said.

'Toh theek hai, jise aacha deal milta hai wahi karenge' Shirishbhai said.

'Hume kaise samaj me aayega ki aap ke builder aachi deal de raha hai aur ham jo mehnet karege uska kya?' blurted Ashokbhai.

Shirishbhai said *'Aare Ashokbhai aisa toh sab jagah hota hai. Usme naee baat kya hai'.*

'Toh aaise me mein kaam nahi karunga' Ashokbhai retorted.

Asifbhai said *'Shirishbhai mein kya bolta hu ke aap Ashokbhai aur humko chhe mahiney dekhane dijiye, phir aap apne builder se baat kijiye'.*

'Hah hah....kyu nahi pehle Ashokbhai ki taraf se karenge phir mein try karoonga. Ye deal zara badi hai isliye mein soch raha tha ki jeetne badi party utna aachhaa…' Shirishbhai said.

He does not have any builder with him right now, thought Vishal.

'Tu theek hai hum chhe mahine try karenge aur phir Shirishbhai aap try kare' Asifbhai concluded. But there was some hesitation in Asifbhai's voice. During the entire session Asifbhai was avoiding Ashokbhai's direction with his posture turning away from him.

After all of them left by 7pm, Vishal thought about the entire session with all his fingertips touching each other and reclining on his chair with his eyes closed.

Kaka thought now Vishalbhai should not be disturbed and he would need tea in some time.

Vishal was thinking furiously….

Journey of a Broker

What is it that was bothering Asifbhai about Ashokbhai. Ashokbhai was not cordial with Asifbhai but so was he with anyone. Ashokbhai knew Asifbhai for some time. Asifbhai did not like Ashokbhai's way of working that was clear. Asifbhai was people's person whereas Ashokbhai was technocrat. Both were opposite ends but together made a good team. Asifbhai would not trust Ashokbhai in any deal and Ashokbhai needed to deal in his own way. Ok then Asifbhai wanted to be with Ashokbhai while he was approaching the builder. 'That's it', Asifbhai was disappointed not being invited to the builder. Instead Ashokbhai called Vishal. Vishal was not so much interested in going to the builder so he thought he would tell Asifbhai to go along with Ashokbhai and Shirishbhai. He decided when Ashokbhai calls up he would decline gently and suggest Asifbhai's name.

Well that happened the next day.

After two days Asifbhai and Manoj came in at 7pm.

Asifbhai was happy and said, *'Vishalbhai aapne aachha sujav diya. Aaccha hua mein chala gaya...haa aap aate toh aur bhi aachha hotaa.*(Vishal smiled from inside) *Lekin builder Navinbhai mujshe milke bahut khush huve. Unhone muzhe chawl malikse nipatne ko kaha. Ashokbhai ke builder aache nikale'.*

As if all Ashokbhai's acquaintance are *'khaddus'* like him.

Vishal gave a smile externally this time but said nothing.

'Chai bolu sabke liye' asked kaka.

'Aare nahi pehle Ashokbhai ko to aane do phir bolna, aur is baar paise mein doonga kaka' jolted Asifbhai.

Vishal thought Asifbhai is very happy and good that I sent him.

Asifbhai was explaining about Navinbhai the builder. He was a big builder and has done some township at Mira road and done lots of small projects here and in Pune. He had good financial backing.

In some time Ashokbhai came with his sardonic smile and sat quietly.

'Kaka ab chai boliye sab ke liye' Asifbhai said.

Ashokbhai said, *'aaisa lagta hai ki project aacha laga Navinji ko. Phirbhi mein dusare builder ko mil leta hu'.*

'Aare nahi Ashokbhai, mujhe lagata hia ki Navinbhai souddha kar lenge' Asifbhai said.

Ashokbhai said in his serious tone, *'hame ek hi par bharosa nahi karna chahiye'.*

Pause. Asifbhai was getting little restless.

Vishal intervene, *'theek hai na Ashokbhai, lekin hum pehle preference Navinji ko denge'.*

'Yeh theek hai Vishalbhai, hain na Asifbhai', spoke Gaattu who was helping kaka to place tea for everyone.

'Theek hai', Ashokbhai said.

The topic changed to Navinbhai the builder and went on and on......

Vishal was thinking if Ashokbhai knew so many good builders why was he not successful or big.

Why does he come to people like us compare to Navinji. There has to be some mystery behind it.

Asifbhai would know.

Any way they were forming a good team. Manoj was very helpful in delivering all the documents to and fro between builder, him, Ashokbhai and Shirishbhai.

Shirishbhai also commented once that Navinji is good builder.

Manoj used to accompany Ashokbhai to registrar and municipal offices to help him. Ashokbhai was very happy with Manoj.

At one time Ashokbhai 'the *khaddus*' praised Manoj.

This was the topic for Asifbhai to tease Manoj, *'kya Manoj aap to khaddus ke dayna haat hogaye'*.

'Aare nahi Asifbhai, Ashokbhai ko bahut jaankari hai yeh office ki' Manoj was blushing. *'Manoj, aap bhi seek lena, Ashokbhai ko bahut knowledge hai iss sab ki. Woh to stocks ke bareme bhi......'* Asifbhai stopped suddenly.

Vishal looked up at Asifbhai's embarassment but immediately turned to Manoj.

He diverted the topic and asked, *'Manoj aur kya baaki hai dene ki liye'.*

'Bas ab kuch nahi... bas ek baar chawl malik se meeting karni hai' said Manoj.

'Hah woh meine baat ki hai aur meeting parso shukrawar jumme ki din rakhi hai. Navinbhai se mere baat hogayi

hai' Asifbhai said recovering. It was after almost 5 months that the meeting took place.

So it was on a Friday the meeting took place at Navinji's office. All were present, Ramprasad Gupta the *chawl* owner, Shirishbhai the broker Guptaji had hired, Manoj, Vishal, Asifbhai, Ashokbhai and Navinji himself.

First all details were to be checked. Navinji had his architect along with his lawyer and his chartered accountant. Ashokbhai knew every one of the associates of Navinji. Ashokbhai and Vishal had met 4 days previously to arrange the documents in proper order. The documents were intact and arrange in files. The originals were with Guptaji.

Navinji's team sat with Vishal and Ashokbhai and did the entire paper work. The draft for the development agreement was ready but had to be checked. The papers were exchanged and the process had begun. Tea, coffee and snacks were served intermittently by Navinji's staff. It took about 2 hours to complete the paper work. The matter which remained was amount to Guptaji and compensation to tenants and brokerage.

Navinji said the amount to be paid to tenants would be about 80 percent and remaining 20 percent would be of Guptaji as per the norm. Also Guptaji would get lump-sum amount along with 2 flats of 2 BHK and 2 flats of 1 BHK which would be of his choice. Shirishbhai said he also needed to have one flat of 2 BHK apart from the brokerage as he was the main broker of seller. Navinbhai denied it and said it was not possible. He would get the equal brokerage as others and if he wants anything extra he should take it from seller. i.e; Guptaji.

Guptaji said, *Shirishbhai I would pay half brokerage from my side'*. Shirishbhai insisted on full brokerage but Guptaji said it is the right amount and asked Navinji to allow Shirishbhai to sell more flats. Navinji said I cannot promise that as I need to sell the flats as and when I get customers and if Shirishbhai do not get any customers then he would be stuck. He said anybody can get customers for him and of course brokerage along with it. But Shirishbhai would be given preference if any dispute arises. Shirishbhai very reluctantly agreed.

The amount had to be decided but he needed a weeks' time to decide as he has employed professionals to value the market rates.

Payment to Guptaji and tenants would be done as per units and negotiation with tenants. The range was fixed between 20 to 25 lakhs, i.e; if 20 lakhs then 80% i.e 16 lakhs to tenants and remaining 4 lakhs to Guptaji. Also Guptaji was supposed to get 10 crores lumpsum. All brokerage would be given at the final payment.

Ashokbhai said Navinji should pay brokerage periodically at the start, then in the middle and then at the end.

Navinji said, *'Ashokji have faith in me. I would not run away with your brokerage. I would stay here for more than 3-4 years for this project and you can ask any brokers in the market'.* Ashokbhai said it is not the question of faith but value to the work done by them. He had complete faith in Navinji otherwise he would not have come to him.

Navinji said he needed to arrange finance from all his sources and agreed to pay part brokerage of 1 lakh each and then the remaining brokerage at the end. But 1 lakh would be given after all the tenants are settled with the amount. Everybody agreed.

So the deal was done. Only the amount was yet to be agreed and filled in the agreement. That happened after 5 days at the same place. All agreements were drawn and signed after checking and rechecking.

'Soudda ho gaya aakhir me' Asifbhai said

Navinji gave 25 lakhs as token money to Guptaji and to everybody's surprise twenty five thousand to each broker. Everybody was delighted.

This was something nobody had expected but Vishal understood it. Navinji needed to sell the flats in future so this is his investment for that.

Navinji was a very shrewd person with a sweet tongue.

Chapter 5
Deal gone sour

After Navinbhai's office Guptaji and Shirishbhai went separately while all other four brokers came to Vishal's shop. This time nobody needed to tell *Kaka* to order for special tea.

It had become a sort of routine to meet every alternate day at Vishal's shop and discuss the matter. Everybody had become fond of *Kaka* too.

Asifbhai said *'Mein ek do din mein Shirdi jayoonga Baba ke paas'*.

Manoj said *'mein bhi aaoonga Asifbhai'*.

'Aare Vishalbhai aap bhi aajaaiye, Ashokbhai aap bhi' Asifbhai said.

Vishal said *'Asifbhai mein yeh sab manta nahi hu per theek hai mein aajaonga. Lekin kal nahi parso rakhiye'*.

Everybody turned to Ashokbhai.

Ashokbhai said *'Ok lekin wohi din wapas aana hien toh'*.

'Aare Ashokbhai, savere jaldi nikalenge aur raat tak wapas. Gaadi hire karenge' Asifbhai said. So it was decided that everybody will go to Shirdi. They had good time and even Ashokbhai was looking happier. He also sung few of old *hindi* songs. Vishal thought this is a good way of spending time and getting close. He still wondered about Ashokbhai's past, but he decided not to probe it today.

So it was almost a year and the progress was slow comparatively. Navinbhai had bought almost 70 per cent of *'kholis'*.

The next 30 per cent had come to a standstill. Shirishbhai and Guptaji were getting restless and tense with every passing week. Guptaji even came to Vishal's shop to discuss the matter.

All were present.

Shirishbhai said *'Navinbhai ek dum thanda gir gaye hai'*.

'Mera lump sum amount ki bhi bat nahi kar rahe hai' Guptaji said.

'Aisa raha toh taklif ho jayegi' Shirishbhai said.

'Mujhe lagta hai Navinbhai shayad koi taklif mein hai' Asifbhai said.

'Aisa hai toh hame batana chahiye, hum dusre kisi ko dhundenge' Shirishbhai said.

'Aise kaise aap dusre ko dhundenge?' Asifbhai retorted.

'Main ne Navinbhai se baat ki hai. Unhone thode din baad mujhe phone karne ke liye kaha hai' Ashokbhai said.

'Toh main dusre ko dhundna shuru kar du?' Shirishbhai said.

Asifbhai said *'Kya Shirishbhai…. Guptaji inko samjhaiye zara. Itna paisa dalne ke bad koi chhod deta hai kya?'*

Guptaji said calmly *'Asifbhai, main ne yeh faisla mere bachon ke khilaf liya hai. Agar kuch gadbad hoti hai, toh voh mujhe maaf nahi karenge'*.

Journey of a Broker

Asifbhai says *'Aisa kuch nahi hoga Guptaji, aap chinta mat kijiye. Ashokbhai unhe phone karne wale hai. Toh hum sab ek bar unhe mil lenge. Kyun Shirishbhai, thik hai?'*

Guptaji continued saying calmly, *'Mujhe dusre investment bhi karne hai. Aur yeh chawl kab tutegi aur naya kab banega?'*

Ashokbhai said *'Ab tak jitney bhi kam Navinbhai ne kiye hai, voh sare achche aur successful huye hai'.*

Vishal said, *'Toh thik hai, Ashokbhhai hum sab ko bata denge khabi Navinbhai ke office mein milna hai'.*

After Guptaji and Shirishbhai departed, Manoj asked *'Sab ko aur ek chai bolu?'* Asifbhai said *'ha ha, bolo'.*

Nobody spoke till the tea was placed in front of them. Manoj said *'Ashokbhai mein Navinbhai ko milkar aaun?'*

Ashokbhai said that Navinbhai is not in Mumbai and is right now in Pune.

Vishal thought that Ashokbhai had done his homework and was hiding something from Guptaji and Shirishbhai. It will be revealed in some time.

Vishal and Asifbhai exchanged glances and understood not to speak till Ashokbhai revealed. Ashokbhai said after finishing the tea, *'inke dusre project mein problem chal rahi hain, isliye koi booking nahi ho rahi hai. Voh khud thode pareshan hai. Unhone mujhe bola hai shayad chche mahine deri ho jayegi'.*

Manoj said *'Shirishbhai toh rukenge nahi. Voh toh hungama karenge'.*

Vishal said, *'Agar karenge, toh bhi kuch fayda nahi hoga. Sabki gaadi bich mein atki hui hai'.*

Asifbhai said *'Haa yahi bat hai, aapne sahi kaha'.*

And then he looked at Ashokbhai.

Ashokbhai nodded his head.

Vishal said , *'Vaise bhi Shirishbhai ke pas dusra builder nahi hai. Guptaji yeh jante hai, isliye voh yaha hume milne aaye thay'.*

Ashokbhai and Asifbhai nodded their head thoughtfully.

Vishal could again join the dots correctly.

Everyone departed except Manoj whom Vishal had held back.

Vishal said, *'Manoj, tujhe Navinbhai ke sab project malum hai na?'*

Manoj said, *'Ha, malum hai. Ek bar main Puna bhi gaya tha Ashokbhai ke sath'.*

'Toh tu do din mein mujhe saari jankari laake dega. Kal chahe toh tu Puna jake aa. Yeh rakh paise tere paas'.

'Aare aare... nahi Vishalbhai, mere paas hai. Chahiye toh aap se mang lunga'.

Vishal said *'thik hai, tu ab jaa'.*
Vishal's mind was racing.

He thought let me decide after Manoj gets the report.

'ಓಶಿ, voh savere agreement rakha tha voh kaha rakha hai?'

After 2 days in the evening, Manoj came little tired and sad.

'Ha Manoj bolu, kya bolte ho??' After making Manoj comfortable.

Manoj said *'Vishalbhai sab jagah kaam band hai aur koi booking bhi nahi ho rahi hai. Sirf Mira road ka project chal raha hai, voh bhi bahut aahista. Pune men toh supervisor bhi nahi hai site per. Mujhe unke office jaana pada. Unke contractor bhi waha khada tha apne payment ke liye. Navinbhai mile nahi aur meine koshish bhi nahi ki jaisa apne bataya vyaise'.*

'Achha achha….' Vishal assured.

'Manoj tumhne bahut achha kaam kiya hai. Tum ab ek din aaram karo. Humhe parso Navinbhai ko milna hai unke office mein'.

As said time and day everybody had gathered at Navinbhai's office.

This time he was alone with his accountant.

He came straight to the point after subdued session of tea and biscuits.

'Dekho Guptaji, jaise ke aap jante hai, aaj kal market bahut tight ho gaya hai hum logo ke liye. Finance milna mushkil ho gaya hai, phir bhi main sab tarah se try kar raha hu. Aap ko mein request kar sakta hu ki aap thoda der sabar karenge toh behter hoga'.

Shirishbhai spurted out, *'Lekin agar aapko paise nahi mile toh kya hoga?'*

Vikas winked and thought this is not going good. Why can't he be quiet for sometime.

Silence for few seconds.

Guptaji said *'Navinbhai aap chhee mahine me intazaam kar payenge?'*

Navinbhai said calmly *'Dekheye hum aaisa kissi ko batate nahi hai, lekin hum aise situation mein hai isliye bata raha hu. Mere sab project mein town planner aur municipality se dikkat aa rahi hai. Yeh naye ruling ki wajah se sab builders ki hawa tight hu hai. Lekin mera Mira road ka project bilkul clear hai lekin waha booking nahi hu rahi hai. Aap sabhi brokers ko meine project ki details bhejhi hai. Manoj ne diye rahenge aap sabhi ko. Usse mera kam chal raha hai lekin aahistase'.*

'Lekihin agar nahi huva toh hum kya karenge?' Shirishbhai quizzed.

'Aise nahi hoga Shirishbhai, mein is field me bahut utar chadav dekhe hai. Property mein kabhi agar sahi tarah ke se paise lagavoh tuh nuksaan nahi hota hai. Guptaji mujh pe vishwas kijiye, meine bhi toh paise lagaye hai. Mere paise phi toh phasey hai aapke saat. Aur aapke paise mein de doonga. Naye DCR ruling ka baad bhi mein aapko utnahi de raha hu jo hamne tay kiya tha. Isme mujhe nuksaan hai lekin deri ki wajah se mein nuksan aapne pe leh raha hu'
Navinbhai said looking at Ashokbhai.

Ashokhbhai and Vishal both nodded.

'Lekin guarantee kya hai?' asked Shirishbhai.
This time Navinbhai said in a slow and deliberate tone with lot of sternness in voice. Nobody thought Navinbhai could talk like this.

He said *'Shirishbhai mein aapko aise bolu toh, jaoo jo karna hai kar lo. Aap mera kuch nahi bigaad sakte. Ye project mein jo koyi naya builder aayega usse bhari matra mein mujhe paise dene padange kyoki mein itna investment karne ka baad aasani se nahi chodonga. Mujhe agar nuksan bhi honga toh mein utha lunga, lekin Guptaji ki haalat patali ho jaayengi. Toh Shirishbhai aap zara shaant bhaitiye aur mujhe mera kaam karne dijiye. Yeh toh Ashokbhai ki wajah se mein apse baat kar raha hu'.* Navinbhai was cooling down.

He further said with his usual sweetness *'Muzhe Guptaji ki nijhi halat malum hai. Mein mere taraf se unko koyi nuksaan nahi hone doonga'.*

Ashokbhai said *'Yeh sahi kah rahe hai Guptaji'.*

Shirishbhai was about to say something when Guptaji said with his hand in front of Shirishbhai, *'Theek hai Navinbhai mein aur che se saat mahine rukta hu'.*

Navinbhai said *'Mein aapko hafte bhar mein ek crore dena ka intazaam kiya hain. Aur sabhi ko aur pachees hazar brokerage bhi de raha hu. Theek hai Asifbhai'.*

Shirishbhai said *'Aap thoda aur brokerage nahi de sakte hai Navinbhai'.*

'Nahi… agar zyaada chahiye toh aakhir me lelijiye. chale ga?'

'Nahi nahi theek hai theek hai…Navinbhai….'

'Ha aur ek chai de sakta hu…' said Navinbhai smiling.

Everybody laughed.

Vishal admired Navinbhai for his cleverness and maturity in handling everybody.

But after few months it was not going very well. Indeed property market was affected everywhere.

Only cash rich builders were able to sustain the flak.

Guptaji had taken ill and was not keeping well. Shirishbhai used to call Vishal with some reason or other and keep telling him, *'yeh deal barabar se nahi jaa rahi hai. Agar mera builder hota to aisa kabhi hota hi nahi'.*

Vishal said to wait and watch for agreed time. But Shirishbhai used to call him almost every alternate day with his set of 'logic'.

Chapter - 6
Mr. Ashok I. Lalka

Mr. Ashok Indravan Lalka looked older than his fifty four years of age. Once, he had a dynamic personality and no nonsense attitude going along with it. He had a very straight forward nature to the level of being rude to others. But he was never rude but just technically right. He always thought why people take so much time to understand and why do not they use their brains!!! Well this attitude started when he was twenty three years old and continued till he turned thirty eight. Well the reason he started looking from others' point of view came about hard way.

The story of Mr. Ashok Lalka was something like this.......
His father Mr. Indravan Lalka was a small time trader in fodder (food material for buffaloes and cows) for large stables in Jogeshwari – Goregaon region dominated by '*UPites*' and '*Biharis*'. He was not educated and was not much for it. His opinion was why waste time in education instead of earning money; the earlier the better. So sometimes young Ashok was taken with his father to many stables. Initially it was fun to watch the buffaloes and cows at close quarters with occasional boost of sweet milk or '*lassi*'.

Later on it led to boredom to get tagged along. Eventually it came to 'making-a-ruckus' out of it and forcing his father to leave him home. Instead young Ashok found interest in studies especially figures. He was good with figures and could solve maths faster than his peers. His father thought his skill was being wasted there.

Anyway, when he turned nineteen and was finishing his graduation in commerce, he was forced to join his often ill father. He had to go to about 4 to 5 stables in a day including Sundays. He had to take his father to cancer hospital in the town side for treatment twice a week. This used to consume his energy to no end. Finally after finishing his second year in distinction (he was third in the university) he had to give up studies.

It was tough for young Ashok to handle the pressure as he had two elder sisters to marry off. At twenty three years he had grown highly intolerable with small and silly things. His family could not understand him. Adding to it was his father demise. He got married at the age of twenty eight (old in his community) to a very composed girl named Usha aged twenty one from poor background. She had a very calming effect on him but only for occasional and shorter periods. Well eventually the calmness increased to longer periods as he grew older.

He had left trading in fodder (criticized by his father to no end). He had started trading in equity as a daily trader but with little success. He lacked the patience of season trader but that was compensated by his knowledge in other field – real estate.

Journey of a Broker

He had been to the stock broker's office at Goregaon as usual, when he was given the work of an absent agent for registration and stamp duty payment of property. This place was used by other property brokers for networking too. Ashok did that and was paid for it. He thought it was easy to handle this and started taking up this job regularly. He got interested in the administrative part and eventually technical aspect of real estate. In fact he became so good at it that property brokers started taking advice form him and he started earning regular income from it. He then gradually got elevated to become a property broker. He used to go to any length to find the answer for any technical and legal aspects of property matter. He liked being the specialist – problem solver, kind of person which caressed his ego to no end. He was known as *'khaddus dimagh'* in sub registrar office which eventually became only *'khaddus'*. In fact he was once called by a sub registrar to his office to solve some complicated matter of an old document. He had earned his reputation as one of the finest minds in property market. He eventually knew property matter like the 'back of his hand'. His visiting card showed techno-legal consultant in bold letters as to compensate for his incomplete education. He showed less emotion and what showed out was only rudeness and intolerability. It was intoxicating at times but used to fulfil his burning desire of being an expert. His clothing sense always used to be at the mark of a management person in some corporate office.

He was growing leaps and bounds in property brokerage and was elevated to doing land deals apart from retail residences and shops. His ego was not satisfied with little success in stock trading. He used to trade with lot of misplaced sentiments in market.

He had earned a reputation with builders' too and was often a sought-after person in their circles.

Once this builder by the name of 'Krishna Developers' had summoned Ashokbhai. He had asked

Ashokbhai to help in the technical matter of land deal at Borivali region. It was a township project. It was regarding the titles of the land. They had a lot of irregularity and missing documents. After that the approved plan was not coming from municipality despite a reputed architect on the job. Ashokbhai did all the work from meeting the owners of land and endless rounds of municipal offices. He had solved one more tedious case and had earned one flat from the builder as per the deal.

During this time Ashok and Usha also had good fortune to be blessed with a baby girl after 7 years of marriage. Ashok now 38 years changed overnight when he took the baby in his hand. He could not describe the feeling but it was the first and last time Usha noticed tears in his eyes. He said to Usha that she is our *'Lakshmi'*. The daughter named "Purvi" was the darling of the father and the only one who dictated the iron man of the house hold with her finger. Everybody would tease Ashok behind his back that he was 'lady follower'. His relatives like his sisters started noticing rare streaks of happiness on his face. Later after 3 years, again they were blessed with a son.

He had a bad experience of land deal once where at the end of the deal he came to know about 9-10 brokers involved. It was a chain of brokers who had come via acquaintance or referred people casually and had lined up for money at the last minute. Nobody understood anything about the property matter but very eager to get their share of money at the end of deal. All these people had come together at the time, the meeting was fixed. It never happened as many of disputes erupted among themselves and good deal was lost. This happened twice with Ashokbhai and he refused participating in deals which came 'via – via – via' some unknown people. He did only land deals which involved not more than three to four brokers and that was rare.

After doing pretty well and earning loads of money he was well respected in the property circle of western suburbs. This lasted for about ten to fifteen years or so when he turned fifty. He had met Asifbhai occasionally through the brokers' network and had done one or two deals with him.

His opinion about Asifbhai was one who gets paid only for sweet talking.

His downfall came not with real estate but stocks. He had invested almost everything into stocks which was against the cardinal rule of investing. After the descent of Sensex on the first day he was advised by stock brokers that the fall cannot be more than two days. He had lost half the amount of his portfolio in two days and lost almost everything on the third and fourth day. He had invested majority of his money in small and mid-cap stocks which had taken the maximum beating. Again an aversion to cardinal rule of well diversified portfolio. He saw his entire booty/money vanish in four days flat. This happened when he was at the stock broker's office where Asifbhai had come for his advice with other property broker. He looked paled and Asifbhai noticed it and suggested him to go home. He in fact asked him if he should accompany Ashokbhai. He declined. He collapsed outside the stock broker's office near the staircase when Asifbhai had returned to get back his forgotten property papers. He was rushed to nearby hospital and diagnosed of 'stroke'. He had to be injected with some expensive 'blood anti-clot' solution or he would suffer fatal consequences. There was no time for arrangement of money and Asifbhai had taken the entire responsibility of it and paid for the medicine.

The following days turned to be from bad to worst. He was attended by Usha and his two sisters and brought back to near normal state within fifteen days. Doctor had advised his family members to get him back to his work but Ashok had no inkling to return to work. His mental state did not allow him to get up from the bed for almost two months. He had mild lingering effect of the stroke on the left side of his body. During this entire time Asifbhai was the family's saviour. He used to physically help Ashokbhai and used to talk to him and the family members consistently. He was the strength behind them. Later, he used to frequent Ashokbhai twice or thrice a week. He tried to get Ashokbhai on his feet to work, but to no results. Gradually their financial state deteriorated to the extent of 'hand to mouth' existence. Ashokbhai would not talk for days together and it started affecting Usha's health too.

Once after few months Asifbhai was sitting in front of Ashokbhai's bed, who was reclining on it; Asifbhai said, 'Ashokbhai, zara apne bachchon ka toh sochiye. Purvi bitiya ab badi ho rahi hai aur parso mujhe bol rahi thi ki, "Asif chacha, aap mere liye kahi kam dekhiye." Ashokbhai mujhe yeh sunkar bahut bura laga. Aapke pas toh property ka itna knowledge hai aur bahut sare mere jese broker aur builders ko aap ki zarurat padti hai. Aap mere saath chaliye, hum naye se kam shuru karenge. Main kal aata hun, aur aap ko le jata hun. Kal hume Sureshbhai builder ke pas jana hai. Ushaben aap Asokbhai ko kal das baje taiyaar rakhiye.' Asifbhai left after few hesitating moments. Ashokbhai was silent for the entire afternoon and night. He declined his food. Next day he was ready to join Asifbhai for work. Usha and family had smile on their faces after almost 6 months.

The relationship between these two elderly friends was beyond anybody's understanding and thus began the second innings of Ashokbhai.

After a couple of years, Asifbhai had got the proposal from Vishal which he thought would interest Ashokbhai.

He told him, *'Ashokbhai yeh redevelopment ka project hai aur yeh jo Vishal hai, voh sahi bandha lagta hai. Ek bar milne mein harz nahi hai.'*

After meeting Vishal two-three times he said, *'Asifbhai, Vishal bahut aage tak jaayega…woh labhi race ka ghoda hai.'*

Chapter 7
Boora Waqt ....Lessons

'Saali nazar lag gayi humsab ko. Boora waqt chal raha hai hum sab ka.....'Asifbhai was saying, 'aur yeh Shirishbahi ne toh itna pareshaan kar rahkaa hai ki lagta hai unko bol do joh karna hai karle. Unke saat ek bhi deal karunga nahi agese'.
Manoj said, 'Voh toh dhamki bhi de rahe they mujhe, ki court mein jaaonga mein....' Vishal said, 'Aisa kuch nahi karenge voh'.
Ashokbhai said, 'Sab jagah pe yahi halat hai. Is mein koi kuch nahi kar sakta, phir bhi Navinbhai sab tarah se try kar rahe hai. Unhone Guptaji aur unke do beto ko office mein bulaya tha. Un se aur thoda waqt manga hai'.
Asifbhai said 'Thodi samajhdari dikhani chahiye Shirishbhai ko'.
Manoj said 'Unke samajh ke bahar hai'.
After everybody left, Vishal analyzed the situation. If the situation continues this way it would be hazardous to him. There was a lull in the market; only few shops under him were on rent. One or two shop owners were thinking of selling them.
When he was thinking about all this, his eyes fell on the magazine "Property Times". He had read in this fortnightly magazine that the builders and investors were in a severe liquidity crunch. The customers were waiting for clear picture

to emerge and sitting on the fence while developers were trying out new schemes to attract the fence sitters. He thought about Navinbhai who was better placed than other builders. He had also seen an ad of Navinbhai's projects in the magazine. There was an ad regarding real estate management, finance and marketing course conducted by the magazine. He thought he would like to meet this property magazine people.

Kaka saw Vishal in his typical thoughtful reclining pose on

chair with fingertips touching each other.

"Time for tea".

Vishal was thinking about Navinbhai; what kind of a person he might be in troubled times. He had a vague idea in his mind since few days about his business model and thought he would approach Navinbhai for his advice. He called Navinbhai's office and got an appointment for the next day at 11a.m. He thought he would be the first appointment for Navinbhai for the day. He prepared for next day's appointment.

Next day he was at Navinbhai's office sharp at 11a.m. Navinbhai was on the phone for a couple of minutes and then he called Vishal inside. Vishal entered the cabin receiving a very warm smile.

'Ao Vishal aoo baitho, chai piyoge? Meri chai abhi ati hogi'.
'Thank you, mein piyunga' Vishal said.

'Ashokbhai tumhari bahut tarif karte hai aur Ashokbhai bewajah kisi ki tarif nahi karte. Bolo, mein kya kar sakta hun tumhare liye?'

Vishal said, receiving his cup of tea in front of him, *'Mein aap se kuch salah lena chata hun'*. And Vishal explained his idea to Navinbhai. Navinbhai heard him out with complete silence. He did not even touch his tea. After listening to Vishal he drank his tea slowly and thoughtfully. After his tea Navinbhai said, *'Idea toh umda hai lekin aap ko execution mein mehnat aur samajhdari dikhani padegi. Kyunki tumhare business model ke liye execution bahut strong honi chahiye'*.

Vishal said *'Achche execution ke liye mere pas achcha infrastructure hona chahiye jaise ki human resources, property experts, software, networking aur jagah. Aur iske liye mujhe funding lagegi'*.

Navinbhai said *'Funding se jyada aap ki core team bahut achchi chahiye'*.

'Lekhin paisee nahi honge toh team kaise banegi' asked Vishal.

Navinbhai waited for few seconds before replying *'Agar aapke paas experience aur knowledge ho ton aapke paas paise bhi aajayenge. Kyuki Saraswati, Lakshmi ko kheechti hai, Lakshmi Saraswati ko nahi kheechti. Lakshmi toh chanchal hoti hai Vishal, voh yaha se vaha ghumthi rahathi hai. Use baandhne ki liye Sarswati (knowledge) yaa experience chahiye'*.

'Mein samjha nahi Navinbhai...'

Navinbhai started discourse to his willing disciple. He explained that money should not be chased but only respected. Do not go after it. Let it come after you. If you run after it would always run from you. Lots of people do *'Lakshmi puja'*, what do they get......... only *'prasad'*.

To attract money you have to make people pay you. They will pay you only if you have experience or knowledge like we give more money and respect to a specialist doctor. You have little experience and knowledge but that can be compensated by a strong core team comprising of property specialists. *"Paisa toh haat ka meil hai"*.

Vishal asked *'lekin paise banana ke liye paise nahi lagte??'*

'Bilkul nahi...always remember "wealth is not earned but created". Aisi cheez banaoo yaa aisa kaam karo jo paisa kheeche. You have customer centric business model, so you are on the right track. Sachin Tendulkar aur Amitabh Bacchan ke paas paisa unke talent ki wajas se aata hai naaki unke shakal aur niji zindagi se. Mere paas investor aur financier mere shakal dhekhar nahi aate, per mera experience aur knowledge dekh kar aate hai. Unhe me fayada dilaate hu iss liye aate hai. Bus apni team banana mey aur customer jootaane pe mahnet karo aur Vishal iske liye bahut kucch khona bhi pad sakta hai. So be ready for it'.

Navinbhai continued *'Iss market ke samay mey aachi team banana mushkil ho saatkta hai, lekin mushkil samay hi aap ki pariksha hoti hai. Agar aap ye abhi kar lete ho toh agey aapko easy ho jayega'.*

Vishal was silent for almost more than a minute for his brain to absorb all, like a blotting paper.

He waited for more.

See to it that you and your team members have same aim other wise it would be like *'haati ka jod'* advertisement of *'fevicol'* where two elephants are moving in opposite direction; going nowhere, Navinbhai concluded.

Vishal said after a long pause *'Aapne mere kitni madat ki hai Navinbhai. Mein aajka din bhulunga nahi. Aapne mujhe bahut kimti salaah dee hai'.*

Navinbhai said standing *'Aare yaha sab salaah dene aate hai, lene nahi. Mujhe bhi tumse baat karke bahut aachha laga. Ashokbhai ne mujhe kaha tha ki Vishal mein bahut potential hai,voh bahut aage tak jayega.....aur mein bhi unse sahmat hu'.*

Vishal instinctively bend and touch his feet...

'Kabhi koi zaroorat pade toh aajanaa....' Navinbhai embraced him.

Vishal knew after leaving the office that Navinbhai meant advice, not money!!

Indian real estate stories

Vishal was at "Property Times" magazine's office. It was a very modest office of not more than 150 square feet on the ground floor of an old building.

On the far corner of the room were two sets of a table and chair with lots of papers, files and latest copies of magazines around. One set was empty and the other chair was occupied with an elderly person of about 68-70 years of age. He had very rugged features with little shaky movements and voice. He had experience written all over him. This man was considered to be a legend in real estate sector. He was giving instructions on the phone and waved his hand to the opposite chair to Vishal.

Vishal sat till the phone conversation was over.

The veteran did not ask anything but, gave an enquiring glance.

Vishal introduced himself and said he would like to know about the courses being conducted for real estate. He asked him to wait for few minutes as his son is on his way to the office and he would explain all the formalities.

Meanwhile the veteran asked why Vishal wanted to do the courses. Vishal explained that he was a small broker and is exposed to a very small section of real estate. Lots of things are unorganized in this sector and he thought this course may improve his knowledge and helpful in upgrading his skill in real estate. Also "Property Times" was doing a very commendable job in organizing this sector. With their magazine he could understand the real estate better and well informed. But with recent slow down everybody was affected.

But that would separate the wheat from the chaff, said the veteran. Vishal agreed.

His son came in and the veteran introduced his son to Vishal. He had a pleasant 'roundish' and ever smiling face.

All three were soon talking as old friends. The son introduces himself as Mr. Rajesh Dubey and his father as Mr. Krishna Dubeyji.

Mr. Rajesh was doing his doctorate in real estate finance and was a visiting professor at a private management college. Senior Dubeyji told him to meet whenever he had time and would extend all support. Rajesh gave him all the instructions and procedural formalities about the course.

Vishal had a lot of interaction with them especially with the senior Dubeyj. He came to know that Dubeyji is a civil engineer by profession and was in the construction line for all his life. He started this magazine to make people aware of the real estate sector. He was successful to some extend but would like to reach more and more people like Vishal. He said he was a pro-buyer and they decided the fate of the sector eventually.

He wanted to give a good name to the sector as against assumed bad reputation. He had an appeal in his voice to people who were spoiling the sector and would go to any extent to help a typical family to buy a house with their hard earned money. He hated bureaucrats in government offices, brokers and builders who were responsible for inflating the rates of property; but not everyone. Vishal was introduced to a third person, elder son of Dubeji as Mr. Mahesh Dubey. He was a kind of hub for lot of brokers' network. He was a source of information for lots of happenings in real estate sector. His knowledge about brokers and builders was tremendous and he was in touch with global practices. Vishal was impressed by the Dubey family managing the magazine so well and growing strength to strength with every passing day.

In one of the interactions with all three of them at their new first floor office he talked about his business model, everybody liked it especially senior Dubeyji.

Mr. Mahesh said that it was similar to global consultancy and needed strong execution. Vishal agreed but in Indian context. He told about the need of core team giving reference of Navinbhai.

Dubey family knew about Navinbhai the builder and respected him.

Mr. Mahesh said he would help him in finding and assembling the team. Also Rajesh said he would help in references in sector for arranging the capital in scaling up. Vishal was grateful to them.

Senior Dubeyji asked to be careful while selecting the team members as it would decide the success of his venture. He also said to go one step at a time and not to hurry up in this process.

'Why can't Vishal scale up the business fast?' asked Mahesh to his father.

'Of course, you should know about 'First Fold' concept'.

'What is that?' Vishal asked.

'Well' said senior Dubeyji and started his theory.

When I was a young person studying for my engineering, my father, who was a small time contractor told me of this concept.

"When you go to buy a sari in the shop, the salesman shows your wife so many of them. You select only one of them and the rest are discarded. Well after you leave the shop, the shop owner and the salesman are left with the remaining opened saris to put it back in their package and place, to look fresh again for the next customer.

The opened sari had to be folded properly to look as new. It would always depend on that first fold the salesman makes that would decide the sari's look. If the first fold is not correct whatever you do after that, the sari would not look nice and new and in fact may look as worn-out. So that first fold is very important and a good shopkeeper knows it. My father said each fold is like each step in your construction. Make it wrong and you spoil the structure.

In your case each team member or step in your business is the fold you would be making. So be careful and patient in making it".

Vishal asked after a long... pause, *'What if you realized you were wrong with some steps and how do you rectify it?'*

Dubeyji continued *'Well, firstly you realized you are wrong itself is a wise thing because many companies struggles in this aspect and try many so called "corrective things". What you have to do is simply go back to the wrong fold or step and do it again properly. That's it'.*

There was a long silence before this real estate legend. Nobody had the gumption to ask any thing as it was so beautifully explained with such simplicity. Vishal knew his father would always say not to complicate things in business. He understood the meaning of simplicity only now.

Chapter 8
Diksha

It was bad time for all. The deal was at status-quo even after two and half years. Guptaji had taken ill seriously and fighting for his life. The only good thing was Navinbhai had somehow paid all the tenants and also the share of Guptaji. The brokers had received their remaining 1st installment of brokerage. Future was in status –quo. Shirishbhai and Guptaji's younger son were thinking of filing a court suite against Navinbhai. Navinbhai had taken all the precaution legally with Guptaji and his elder son. So it was only development which had to start but with no money and strict government regulations, Navinbhai had his hands tied. Vishal's NRI friend Rajeev was also delaying his decision of investing and thought to wait for some time or invest in Pune. So it was bad times.....

Meanwhile VIshal thought of his business model feverishly for weeks together and endless teas.

In fact, once Kaka thought of starting a tea stall next to their shop!!

Vishal kept refining his model, meeting Dubeyji and preparing for his real estate courses.

He also met some of the people who Mr Mahesh suggested for team formation.

He thought of calling his friends to his shop and revealing about his plan. He needed their guidance especially of

Ashokbhai and Asifbhai. He knew the outcome of this meeting but thought it is his moral responsibility to inform them.

All of them had grown fond of Diksha.

Infact Diksha was the only the person whom Ashokbhai talked endlessly. This was surprising to all other three friends.

Asifbhai said to Manoj *'Manoj teri jagah ab Diksha beti ne leliya hai'.*

Manoj said *'Asifbhai, Dikshabhabhi hai hee aisii. Mera bhi bahut khyal rakhti hai. Mujhe rakhi ke din bulaya tha aur mast gujarathi khana khilaya tha. Kyu Vishalbhai haina?'*

Asifbhai said *'Aare Vishal apna bhi khana uddhar raha Diksha beti per haa'.*

Ashokbhai smiled and said *'Mein bhi aaunga…'* to everybody's surprise.

After their usual tea session Vishal explained about his new development and his plan and scaling up.

Asifbhai said *'Vishal yeh bahut badi uuchi jhhumpp hogi….'*

Ashokbhai was silent. Manoj could not understand properly.

'Isi liye to aapki madat chahiye…Asifbhai' Vishal said.

Vishal explained that times are changing and real estate is becoming more and more professional. One or two brokers would not survive the race in future and need to come together to form a strong team. Only reputed and professional brokers or consultant will serve the ever demanding customer and end-users.

'Haa yeh baat toh hai….Mujhebhi dikat hone lagi hai…Kabhi kabhi mujhe samaj me nahi aata hai ki customer kya bol raha hai' Asifbhai said.

Ashokbhai said 'Asifbhai hum log budhe ho chale hai….Vishal it is good plan per execution acchi chahiye'.

Vishal said 'isiliye aap ko bulaya hai. Kya aap dono mujhe join karenge?'

Long pause.

Asifbhai said 'Vishal aabhi ye umar me yeh sab nahi kar sakta hu…Mein yehi soch raha tha ki ab mein muluk jaaonga aur waha rahunga. Apni thodi zameen aur dukaane hai udhar. Mera beta bhi vahi rahta hai. Lekin tum jab bhi mujhe bulaaoge mein madat karne ke liye aajaoonga. Yeh mera vadha raha tumse….'

He turned towards Ashokbhai.

Ashokbhai looked at Vishal for some time before speaking. 'Vishal, it is good concept and this is the way to go forward'.

Vishal said 'I was thinking if you could join me as techno-legal head…'

Ashokbhai again taking his time said 'Vishal like Asifbhai I also would not to like to work for somebody at my age after working all my life as self-employed. I like to be freelancer and like Asifbhai I would help you whenever you need me. I *would like to see your progress at close quarters'* concluded Ashokbhai affectionately.

'Do you think Ashokbhai this is the right thing to do?' asked Vishal.

Here is Ashokbhai's story from his own mouth....

See Vishal. I earned lot of money in my prime time due to my knowledge and experience in this field. I got carried away and lost almost all my money in stock trading thinking I knew everything. Knowledge and experience do get money but to retain it needs wisdom which very few people have. Asifbhai knows about my career but has never mentioned it to anybody about it. That's his maturity and ethics.

Asifbhai was looking down.

Ashokbhai continued *'Lot of property brokers themselves do not know so much about this sector.*

How they would serve customers? Again this sector is so ambiguous with lot of 'ifs and nots'.

Yours is the step in right direction and help the customers'.

Then Ashokbhai said something which stunned everybody and knew what this person is worth.

He said,

Any business, field or sector is driven by their consumer or end-users. Though she may be a small or tiny person but together they decide the drift of the market. The entire market is given direction by this end-user.

End-user is very lazy and likes everything to be served on platter or rather spoon-fed.

Journey of a Broker

The multi billion dollar companies decide their strategies, marketing, financing, operations and other parameters of business on this single 'almost non existence' end user.

This end-user has lever of fate of these giants but sadly unaware of its 'ephemeral power'.

Everybody was silent…..

Customer will become aware with advanced information technology and would demand certain professionalism from you in coming years. You would see lot of small time brokers becoming extinct. You are right in your prediction. You should keep the model improving with time. I would refer you to some people for finance. One of them is CA by profession and arranges corporate financing for entrepreneurs. His name is Atul Bhat, he will help you understand the concept of finance. I will talk to him in 1 or 2 days.

Asifbhai talked of his experience,' *Mein yeh jaanta hu ke bahut saare brokers aapne fayade ke liye deal karvate hai. Woh bahut kuch kharidaar se chupate hai. Woh yeh business ko kharab karte hai. Mere paas technical knowledge nahi hai lekin mein Ashokbhai jaise logo ki madat leta hu. Yeh lalchi brokers deal karvane ke liye kuch bhi kar sakte hai. Yeh log aghe nahi badte. Meree paas abhi bhi das pandhara saal purane customers aate hai unke kisi rishteydar yaa dost ke lekar kyunki unko mujpar bharosa hai. Property dealing aakhir kar bharose pe chalta hai. Mujhe toh ye lagta hai ki bahut saare log property me bahut saare paisee dalte hai.'*

Asifbhai continued. The old system was better when you would get house on lease basis for affordable amount. You do not have to go for buying a house. But as it is an emotional and social issue everybody likes to have one. Just think all the money people earned goes into property and repaying their EMIs. So who is benefited ultimately, the banks and developers. So rich become richer and middle class remains poorer. If government could come out with policy in favour of middle class to give flats on long lease basis so much money would be diverted and used for country's benefit, concluded Asifbhai.

Vishal said *'Dubeyji also says the same thing, some developers want to make profit over profit and there is no end to it'.*

Ashokbhai nodded.

But in materialistic and consumerism age this is not going to happen.

Vishal said *'Can Manoj work for me Ashokbhai?'*

Of course, why are you asking me 'Vishal, ask Manoj himself' said Ashokbhai.

Vishal said *'Meine Manoj ko puchha tha per usne mujhe aapse puchhne ko kaha hai....'* Ashokbhai was touched and said *'Manoj bahut kabil ladka hai lekin tum agar uska khyal rakhoge toh bahaut achha hoga uske liye'.*

Manoj was overwhelmed and said, *'Bolo Vishalbhai kaha aur kaise karna hai…'*
Everybody started laughing……
𝒦𝒶𝓀𝒶 sometimes did not understand why these people keep drinking so much tea and laughing.

It was now time to talk to Diksha about his plan and the development happening. How he was missing her. She had been to her parents place for two days for her younger sister's wedding preparations.
Diksha was not in her element at her parents place. She wanted to go back home. She was missing Vishal. She knew Vishal was thinking about something important. He was not himself for last few days and did not praise her food as he always does. She thought he needs me and once had called to know about him. 𝒦𝒶𝓀𝒶 said he had gone out to meet

somebody and will come back in the evening. She saw him studying in the nights after meal. She did not disturb him knowing he would talk to her when thought the time wqs right. She knew by now not to force him into anything otherwise it would back fire.
She was worried about him because he never looked so tense anytime in his life. She knew he could not sleep for past few days properly. She did not show on her face about it and pretended as if nothing had happened. Only thing which had not changed was morning tea time. He still looked at her

the same loving way he always had been looking at her since their marriage. She felt so complete, so loved …. She was missing him.

Her mother asked her what was the matter. She said nothing but stayed two days as her sister needed her.

Diksha had returned home and informed kaka while returning. Vishal just came from Ashokbhai's place and was informed about Diksha.

He thought he would go early today. He wanted to talk to her so much!!

He left the shop early and reached his house before time. Diksha was busy with the food preparation. She asked him whether she should make tea for him. He refused and asked about the preparation at her parents place. Diksha started talking and could not stop till the food was placed on the table. Vishal thought how happy she was and thought about postponing the discussuion till tomorrow.

Diksha did not ask him anything. She knew he will come when he is ready. That night she slept properly in Vishal's arms. They felt as if they had met after a long time. Vishal also slept properly after a long time. He felt fresh in the morning. He thought this is the right time to tell her. When Diksha came with the tea in the morning, he gave her a loving and affectionate smile. While drinking tea Diksha sensed now it would come. She was ready for it. Vishal started talking about his new business and the idea of scaling up. He talked everything, meetings with Navinbhai, Property Times people, Ashokbhai and Asifbhai. He also informed about Manoj joining him; everything in language which she could understand. She asked some specific questions which she did not understand but was satisfied when Vishal made it simpler.

Vishal thought now is the real test and said *'Diksha I may mortgage the shop and house as we would need the money. In extreme case we would also have to sell them, first house and then shop. It would be a risky step and would take us to higher level or get us down to lowest level. If only she is ready he would like to go ahead'.*

Diksha asked *'why house first and then shop?'*

Vishal said because shop gives us some income and would like to retain as far as possible.

'But that is if we encounter losses?' Diksha enquired.

'Yes, said Vishal, *and it is highly possible in this bad times....'*

Diksha waited for some time and thought more may come.

After long pause Vishal asked *'What do you say?'*

'What should I say, do what you feel is right' said Diksha.

'But if we go down then......' asked Vishal.

Diksha said after a pause that during her marriage to Vishal, my mother had asked my father, how is Vishal, will our Diksha be happy?

Her father had said that if Vishal was even half good as his father Ramnikbhai then we do not have to worry about Diksha.

Diksha continued, *'today I can tell with confidence and pride that my husband is much more and ahead of my father-in-law Ramnikbhai'.*

Vishal was touched and took Diksha in his warm embrace. He had tears in his eyes.

'Mujhme abhi das gunna himmat aagayi hai Diksha....'

Diksha thought how if he never leaves me from his embrace......

Chapter 9
Finance

As decided Vishal was visiting Mr. Atul Bhat the CA suggested by Ashokbhai.

He had gone shopping yesterday with Diksha for formal wears as suggested by Ashokbhai. Ashokbhai had instructed him about formal wears when meeting with any financial person as that creates a first good impression. He winked thinking he hated wearing ties and formal wears.

Diksha was the happiest lot as she would get the opportunity to shop and select dresses for him.

She had already spoken to Ashok uncle about it and understood the requirement.

Ashokbhai had already talked about Vishal to Atul.

Vishal now wearing formal wear with a tie was at Nariman point, the financial hub of Mumbai. He looked around and thought how this world is; how much worth of deal, negotiation and business must be happening here everyday. And at the road side you find people having snacks and mini meals. Mumbai can accommodate all kinds of people. This place had an old worldly charm you may find nowhere else.

He came to Mr. Bhat's office on 2nd floor of solid looking old but well maintained building. A peon opened the door for him. The first thing he noticed was papers, files, folders and stationary all around. It was a typical CA's office. Second thing he felt was coldness in the room because of the air-conditioning. The peon took Visha's visiting card and told him to wait. He went inside a cabinet looking place hidden between some more files and loads of books on the shelf. He would not have notice the door if the person had not opened it.

He was immediately ushered inside.

When Vishal entered inside first thing he felt was extreme coldness in the room which was about more than 200 square feet.

He thought how does this person stay in this cold? He must be from Antarctica!

He received an enthusiastic smile from an enthusiastic person. He was very fair almost to the colour of milk. He would have definitely passed as a foreigner had he not spoken his next sentence.

'Aavo avo Vishal aavo…. Baitho….please be comfortable. Mujhe Ashokbhai ne bataya aapke bare me. Pehle…. kya loge aap chai ya coffee...'

Vishal said with smile *'Pehle thodhi thaand kam kardhenge aap...'*

Atul laughed and said *'Of course of course….sorry Vishal mujhe garmi bardaash nahi hoti'*. Vishal's mind machine had started spurting. He is rich kid probably form rich background. He probably has studied abroad. He is very well settled in his profession probably because of his father. And then he saw this picture frame on the huge table at the side.

There were two men in it. One was resembling the person in front of him but much younger and the other was much older version of the person in front; may be he and his father some time ago.

Around the room were lots of wall photo frames depicting degrees, diplomas and certificates from universities abroad which Vishal was not able to understand.

'Mein aapke liye coffe mangata hu garama garam... kuch khayenge aap...'

'Nahi nahi, coffee chalegi...'

After the formalities Atul came to the point.

'Ashokbhai said you wanted funding for your venture in real estate'.

'Yes, that is right' Vishal said.

'I saw your presentation in the mail and Ashokbhai briefly explained me. But I would like to know from you so I understand the concept clearly'.

Vishal had gone with the presentation so many times. This time he did not have to use the slides, but Atul did refer to it. Atul was no nonsense type but very friendly. He must be as old as Vishal. He would refer by name (probably because of his abroad influence) but it was alright with Vishal because he could relate to him in same way and it was easy that way. In fact when Vishal left he felt he had met some old time friend.

After the presentation Atul said *'Since I know the concept now I would like to quantify your requirement in rupees'*. *'What is that Atul?'* Vishal asked.

'See Vishal, I would like to estimate financial requirement for your project, so we need to quantify the amount. Now for you to start your first branch or franchisee you need how much?' *'I would say approximately 25 to 30 lakhs'* said Vishal.

'I do not think so Vishal. My estimate is 55 to 60 lakhs. But that is preliminary. How much are you contributing initially Vishal?'

'Around 12 to 15 lakhs' replied Vishal

'Did you met your marketing firm and discuss with them you marketing strategy?' asked Atul

'Yes they have given me a budget of 12-15 lakhs'

'Please add at least 10 lakhs to it. That is always the case with them and knowing your marketing requirement you easily need the amount'.

Vishal thought Ashokbhai has sent me to the right person. *'I have already made your financial projection but I needed to concern you before finalizing'.* He passed a set of papers to him written 'Financial projections for Vishal Doshi for 6 months, 1 and 2 years'.

Vishal went to through it and since he was commerce student understood it. But Atul had made it easy for non commerce student. He must be coming across so many people like him.

Vishal corrected some requirement and with his input Atul added some. This went on for at least half an hour and you could see the final draft of typed and written (with pencil) sheet.

'Ok. Vishal so now we are done with the final requirement it would be easy to be specific about the amount' Atul said and order for another round of coffee.

Vishal thought probably he is taking a break.

When they were having coffee Atul came to the point directly.

'Are you aware of the commission you have to pay me Vishal?' This guy does not waste time with anyone.

'No' said Vishal.

'Ok. We take 5 % percent of your entire funding as our fees. That would be around 3 lakhs rupees'.

'Ok' Vishal said.

'So let's add this as our expense to financial projection for the first year'.

Vishal thought he does not waste time as well as figures…..

'The entire projection would include seed funding and angel investing which I would try to arrange' continued Atul.

Vishal asked *'Would you mind explaining different types of funding and what I am supposed to know about it'.*

'Of course, Vishal'.

He loves "of courses"!!

Atul said *'there are different types of funding available according to your requirement'.*

"Jaisa customer, vaisa maal" thought Vishal.

Atul was continuing *'Seed funding is the initial amount needed to start any business. In your case you have 12-15 lakhs. That is seed fund. Next is if you are starting a business where more capital is involved than you need additional funding called angel funding provided by angel investors.*

Angel investors are high net worth individual or small financial companies or simply bank. Chances of you getting money from bank is ruled out which is the case with most of the entrepreneurs. Financial companies do give funds but are very sector specific. They love digital ventures than mortar & brick like yours, though I am trying with few. Your chances of getting funds are more with angel investors. I have short listed few of them'.

'Vishal I would like to tell you about angel investor. These breed are very shrewd people with very high 6th sense. They decide their investment with their instinct. I am not able to understand their logic some times but I have come to believe and respect their instinct in the last 15 years. I some times feel they go with the person's passion or some times simply with the business model. I have failed to understand them fully'.

'How much funding have you arranged till now, if you do not mind asking me, Atul?'

'Of course, of course...not. I think I have done more than 35 to 40 funding in last 10 years. I was with financial funding house for 5 years before that. So you see Vishal..... I would be taking you to at least 5 of them and if nothing works with them then we have to rework our pitch or tweak the model or come out with something which they may appreciate. Mind you Vishal they have a very good business sense and some of them are successful serial entrepreneurs'.

'How do they get profit?' Vishal asked point blankly.

'Well they exit after say 3-5 years with their profit when you take your business to higher level by 2nd round of funding or venture capitalist entering and then may be you would go further and have public offer issues or IPO'.

'And how much profit are they looking for?' asked Vishal.

'Some times they asked pure interest or they would like to be equity partner with you' Atul was saying this with frequently touching his nose.

Vishal thought he is not comfortable talking this and hiding something from me.

'Ok who decides the interest or valuation and the profit part?' Vishal asked.

'Well it is decided between him and you....'

'See Vishal, Atul said, *it is what they see in the business and how much risk they are taking that would decide these things'.*

'Normally how much profit are they looking for?' asking second time.

'Depending on the risk, anywhere between 40 to 300 percent. In fact I have done a deal where they have exited at 500 percent'.

'Ok', Vishal was thoughtful.

So it was arranged to meet the first investor in 2 days at Atul's office.

Vishal was thoughtful the whole train journey back to Borivali.

He did not know when he arrived at the station.

He met Mr.Rajesh Dubey next day to know more about the financing.

Chapter 10
Investor

After two days, he would meet Mr. Bansal. Atul had called him 1 hour early so he could brief him on Mr.Bansal. His brief was as follow,

Mr.Bansal aged about 60 years has come up a hard life. He was a straight forward person and does not like 'beating around the bush' as they say.

He comes to the point and wants others to do the same. He had made very clear to Atul many times over that his time is very precious and would like him to select cases properly before coming to him. He had done some 8 cases with Mr. Bansal till date. Only 4 had been successful. He does not like equity stake in any of his venture and only need to know about the outcome and his share of profit. He is very tough in negotiation.

Vishal was ready and had one request to Atul; not to interfere when it comes to equity or profit margins.

Mr Bansal came exactly 2 minutes before scheduled time. He was ushered in immediately. After the formalities Vishal came to the point immediately, *'Bansalji, I am looking for 45-50 lakhs rupees of funding for my business'.*

Bansalji asked *'Aap kitne paise laga rahe ho?'*

'Baraah se pandhra lakh tak?' Vishal replied.

'Exactly how much 12 …or 15 lakhs…?' Bansalji asked.

Atul was touching his nose or trying to cover his mouth.

'15 lakh rupees'. Vishal said calmly.

'Aur aapka business kya hai samjaiange mujhe?'

Vishal went on explaining the business but taking care not to go into details and add anything irrelevant according to Bansalji's point of view like marketing expense.

Bansalji said, *'Why should I buy property from you? What is so unique about your company?'*

Vishal said, *'we would be catering to middle class people with mid income budget i.e two level above base of the pyramid. By not sticking to one locality as traditional broker does, we could cater to huge market with professional services (with competitive fees) which would be beneficial to property buyer and end-users. My vision is whenever one thinks of property they should think of our company'.*

'And what about the other upper class or luxury and corporate clients? They have big ticket investment or purchasing power.' asked Bansalji.

'They would not come to me without any track record Bansalji. So when our company makes a mark in the market they would automatically come to us. And all the other people who also acquire property otherwise would think of us at least once'. Vishal concluded.

Bansalji was thinking and he took some time before talking. This surprised Atul as he had never seen Bansalji so quiet in negotiations. Atul was thinking Vishal is doing well and Bansalji must have liked the business model.

Bansalji asked *'who would be your team members?'*

This time Atul and Vishal both explained to him about competent team getting assembled.

'How much equity you are willing to give me in your business?' asked Bansalji.

This jolted Atul from his seat...... But Vishal was expecting this.

'No Bansalji. I do not want to part with equity; I like to have only financial arrangement'. Atul thought of running away from the scene..."what is Vishal doing? Has he gone mad?" were the thoughts he was having when Bansalji's next question almost made him faint.

'But I am helping you reduced your risk completely by offering you partnership'. Bansalji said.

How come Bansalji is even talking about equity....was a mystery to Atul?

Say yes and negotiate on the equity, Vishal......Atul was thinking.

Vishal said, *'No Bansalji if you do not mind I do not want to part with equity and that is final. If only you could tell me how much profit are you looking for at the end of say 3 years?'*

'Ok Vishal, I think I would like to have ..... 100 percent profit every year. That would be of course compounded on to the subsequent years' Bansalji said.

'Not more than 30 percent sir...' Vishal said.

Who is dictating the deal here......"Vishal.... Bansalji is the financier not you" Atul was screaming inside his mind. This is not going the right way.

'I like to have minimum 80 percent profit annually Vishal' Bansalji said.

Vishal looked at Atul and after a deliberate pause said, *'Bansalji I would let you know via Atulji'.*

Atul had almost died.

After an embarrassing farewell to Bansalji, Atul sat on his chair with long phew.....

Vishal was smiling.

Atul said *'Do you want finance or no? I mean, Bansalji has never asked for equity to any of his financing till now and when he was offering it to you why did not you take it?'*

'First of all' Vishal said, *'I was expecting Bansalji would offer equity when he asked about team members'.*

'So what Vishal, he is the financier and you are in need of finance, are you not?' asked Atul.

Vishal said, *'Do not worry we would get a better financier'.*

Atul was surprised, *'That means you do not want financing from Bansalji'.*

'No, I do not want financing from Bansalji....' Vishal concluded calmly.

'Ok, Vishal I have lined two-three more financiers next week, so let's give it a try' Atul said matter of factly.

'Ok', said Vishal and departed.

This time Atul was thoughtful...what is Vishal expecting??

Journey of a Broker

He was surprised to get a call form Bansalji asking for update on Vishal's need. Atul now was sure Vishal has done some magic on Bansalji. He did not say anything about rejecting his proposal but said he would let him know in a week's time. Atul could not sleep that night.

Following week they met two more investors. One investor did show interest but said the financial arrangement was not favourable because of risk involved. Another said Vishal should abandon the idea all together.

Next week when Atul called Vishal, he said we have to meet the investor next day at 4.30 pm near Khar station. He would brief on him if he comes 1 hour earlier. It was their fourth investor. Vishal agreed and was there as expected 1 hour earlier.

Atul was sitting in the chauffeur driven car with air-conditioning to full speed. He greeted Vishal formally and suggested we sit at a nearby restaurant since we have some time and he would like to prepare him before the meeting. Vishal agreed with a smile.

When they were seated comfortably and when the air conditioning was to his desired level Atul ordered for 'idli-wada' for both of them.

'Well he said, Vishal I did not know what magic you have with Bansalji, he had called again yesterday enquiring about the proposal'.

Vishal was smiling too long for Atul.

'Well let us concentrate on our present task' and gave a profile of one Mr. I M Mehta. He is a seasoned investor for more than two decades of experience. Nobody has understood his way of investing till now. At least I have not been able to decipher it.

Vishal was interested.

'He stays with modesty with no frills at all. In fact he is placed at Khar for more than 25 years with not a single car when he could afford a BMW & sea-facing flat at Napensea road. He would appear like any other retired person at his age of 62 years but is very active in keeping his health up to mark. He is been successful in almost all his ventures. He has some times asked for huge profit or very little depending on his perception of project. He has huge equity in some companies and little equity in some very successful companies. And mind you it is worth huge amount in crores. He does not churn his portfolio as often as other investors. He has huge stake in some selected listed companies'.

Vishal asked Atul *'Has the investor had any business experience earlier?'*

'Yes, about 20 years back and he still has stake in that' Atul replied.

Vishal smiled in his thoughts.

Vishal was satisfied when tea was place in front of him.

Journey of a Broker

Atul gave a call from his cell to Mr. I M Mehta. After listening on the cell for about few seconds, he disconnected the cell. *"Let's go Vishal".*

They parked the car in front of a thirty year old but well-maintained building. Atul said he hated this old building without a lift.

They climbed three floors to land in front of Mr. Mehta's flat. After catching his breath, Atul rang the bell of the flat which was hidden in the farthest corner. After few seconds, the door was opened by Mr. Mehta himself. He welcomed Atul and Vishal into a spacious living room with optimum but solid and comfortable furniture. After making themselves comfortable, Mr. Mehta said it is he's tea-time now so would they join him.

Vishal said, *"Yes please, tea would do".*

Atul said, *"I would not mind a cold drink"* wiping his forehead.

"As you please, Atul."

After the beverages were placed in front of them by his modest wife, Mr. Mehta involved in small talks till they were consumed.

Atul said *'Mehtaji, Vishal here needs finance for his venture in real estate'.*

Mehtaji said, *'Are you thinking of being a builder, Vishal?'*

'No. no Mehtaji, I am thinking of servicing customers in real estate' Vishal answered.

'Oh....you mean broker or real estate agent' Mehtaji said.

'I am a real estate agent sir, but I want to provide professionalized services in this sector.'
'How you will you do that?' Mehtaji asked.
Vishal explained his model with USP this time in details.
'Ok….how would you reach your customers, Vishal?' asked Mehtaji.
Vishal said, *"Mehtaji I would be outsourcing reputed marketing agency as it would be important to ……….. "* He explained his marketing strategy.
'Uumm… that means you would be investing money into marketing and there is no guarantee of returns for it?' asked Mehtaji. Vishal thought he has caught me.
'Yes, but I treat this investment as a brand building for my company. And brand does carry goodwill and valuation'.
Atul thought, "Very well put".
There was a long pause.
'So how are you going to scale up?' asked Mehtaji.
Vishal explained, *"We have short-listed the regions for our branches. We would be opening our first branch in one of the potential locality and then expanding to second one after we break even with first. The third branch would be franchise or our extension depending on the system refinement. After second or third branch we should have all our systems in place. So we would scale up fundamentally strongly and may be faster with franchisee model".*
Long silence again…..

Atul was getting restless. Vishal looked at him and indicated him to be calm with a long blink. Vishal thought that Mehtaji has liked my business model and would ask me for some financial arrangement. What it would be? Equity or profit? Vishal was thinking this when Mehtaji surprised him by asking, *'Tell me something about you and your background.'*

"*Sona khara cchhe ki nahi?*" thought Vishlal.

He told him about himself and about his background briefly but without hiding anything. Atul was getting bored. He thought,*"I have to look for another financier. This was Mehtaji's polite way of saying "no".*

After along pause, Mehtaji asked Vishal, *"How do you want the arrangement?"* Atul was completely stunned.

Vishal thought, *"Oh! This is a googly for me. He is checking my business aptitude."*

Vishal said taking his own time, *'I would like you to be equity partner in "our" business'.*

'What is your requirement, Vishal?'

Vishal said, *'About 45-50 lakhs apart from 15 lakhs of my own'.*

'Ok, I would have 20 percent equity' said Mehtaji.

"Ok", Vishal said.

Both of them looked at Atul. Atul did not know how to react.

"Ok Atul, you please make the contract and agreement ready. I would release first installment of twenty five lakhs to Vishal in a week's time. Next twenty five lakhs I would

release after three to six months depending on the requirement." Mehtaji said.

"Ok, I will get back to you Mehtaji when I am ready. Vishal will join me too".

They all got up.

"All the best, Vishal" said Mehtaji smiling away.

When they were back in the car, Atul said, *"I do not know what happened there but Vishal I have started to believe that you have some magic wand with you. You know Mehtaji has valued your business to almost 2.5 crores".*

"Oh no Atul, it is just the difference between Lakshmi and Saraswati". Vishal replied.

What, what are you saying?? asked Atul slightly puzzled.

"Nothing important to you Atul. Somebody taught me to respect money and grow cautiously. Not to run for it", said Vishal.

Ohh…. said Atul now completely puzzled.

'So we will meet after how many days Atul….'

'*Give me at least 3-4 days to draw the contract and agreement with all other formalities'* said Atul.

'*Of course, of course…..'* said Vishal taking Atul's words.

Chapter 11
To Boston...

The scene was Vishal and Diksha's new house; morning tea time.

Vishal was saying, *'how different people became my mentors at different times. Asifbhai, Ashokbhai, Navinbhai and Dubey family. Their lessons were so helpful in our growing up. Past three years were very tiring but satisfying. Our 4th franchisee branch at Bandra was a success.*

We already are flooded with so many registrations'.

Diksha said, *'Ha re ha... Mehta (I.M. Mehta) uncle was praising you a lot. He was telling Ashokbhai that aajkal internet ke funding zamane mein aisa funding safe hai mere liye. Manojbhai was so busy and taking care of everybody. Ashokbhai and Asifbhai were smiling the whole session and in fact were so happy to announce that you are going to Boston for a real estate conference. You are going to give a lecture there?'*

'Not a lecture but a presentation. People from all over the world in real estate are attending it. I would be sharing some ideas of mine to expand in real estate sector in emerging markets especially in India'. Vishal said.

'So you would be meeting Rajeev and family in Boston?' asked Diksha.

'Yes I have already spoken to him; he will come to pick me up after the lecture. I may be with him for one day and then return home', Vishal said.

'So…you would be going without me and then roaming all over Boston. How could you do this to me?' Diksha asked with mockingly sensuous mood.

Vishal said, *'Not again Diksha, you already know I am going only for 5 days. I would be taking you all again next time'.*

'Ok baba, I am just teasing you…..Good Asifbhai and Ashokbhai are working together for our Borivali house society redevelopment'.

'Yes, I had a meeting with Navinbhai and he would be doing the redevelopment. The society people had approached me and given the responsibility. I delegated the entire process to efficient hands of Ashokbhai and Asifbhai'.

'Are they really efficient, I mean in big projects'.

'Yes. Yes absolutely. Asifbhai would handle the society members and Ashokbhai the technical and legal aspect. My team also would help them in the process. With Navinbhai in picture it should not be a problem, hoping so'.

'Yes it was a difficult phase for him in Guptaji's case. How is Guptaji now?' asked Diksha with enthusiasm.

'Oh, he is alright. I met him last week to give him his final cheque and to sign all the agreement.

He was very happy. All were present', said Vishal.

Journey of a Broker

'Any way I have to prepare for our lunch; today everybody would be coming and you have a flight to catch at night', said Diksha getting up and hurrying towards the kitchen.

Vishal thought I would finish my work with **the** 'Blue Horizon Capitals' in the afternoon and would be done for this week. I can go to Boston with ease.

He distinctly remembered the first meeting with 'Blue Horizon Capitals'. It was at evening when he had gone to meet their Indian head.

'Blue Horizon Capitals' a.k.a BHC was a PE fund (private equity fund) for real estate sector from USA and interested in Indian market. They were looking out for investment for some time now. Vishal had approached them through Mr. Rajesh Dubey of Property Times. It was their third venture or project in India, two being in Bangalore and Chennai. They have JV (joint venture) with reputed regional developers and contractor. They follow strict guide lines and corporate governance to select the developers; no "hanky panky" business.

Vishal had been to BKC but never at Trade Centre. He had to meet the country head of 'BHC'; a gentleman called Mr. Mohit Ranade. He knew they were punctual with time and so was he. He was present two minutes before time. He was ushered into a well done office. It had 'corporate' written all over it. He was received by the man himself, Mr. Mohit Ranade, a well groomed personality aged late forties or early fifties. He wore a pair of frameless glistening spectacles. Mr Mohit introduced himself and said to please address him as 'Mohit'. He was taken to a small cubicle of not more than 100 square feet. It had all the latest communication gadgets.

'What will you have Vishal?'

'Any thing hot would do'.

'So let's have coffee.'

'Thank you Mohitji. I mean Mohit.'

'Tell me Vishal, Mr Rajesh and Mahesh had told me about your proposal.'

Ok, then both had spoken to him. He had a strong American accent but something along with it which sounds familiar, thought Vishal. He could not place it, but did not speak.

'Vishal we had sent communication to all reputed real estate people in the country to announce our readiness to do business in the country. We have presence in about more than 80 countries and I am in charge of Asian region. Property Times are our old acquaintance. So tell me what proposal you have for us.'

'Aha… now I got it, he has slight Marathi accent with it, thought Vishal.

Vishal said coming to the point *'Thank you for your precious time. I had this proposal with me for more than 3 years.'*

He knew, here no small talk will survive.

He said *'I have project at Goregaon, western suburb of Mumbai for redevelopment. It has been lingering for last three years because of lack of fund with the builder, the reason for which you are already aware. The real estate scene in India is so depressed with liquidity crunch.'*

Mr Ranade was aware of the situation in India and almost everywhere in Asia except for few countries. He knew it was mainly because of US down-turn and European crisis. It was a cyclical sector and cyclical effect on economy especially in India. Indian equity market was affected with FII inflows or outflows and this affected other economic fronts. Though India was agrarian (agricultural) country, it was undergoing rapid urbanization compare to any other emerging country except may be China. Urbanization was inevitable in a progressing country where infrastructure and property sector forms the main ingredient. It is this need which India was coping up with. He also knew this might be good opportunity for 'BHC' to invest but with only strong fundamental projects. So he needed to be convinced about the project fundamentals and not only it's potential.

Vishal continued, *the project has got all the settlement done with tenants, so that work is already taken care of. The issue is with the planning stage where the builder is not getting his plan approved because of new rulings in amended municipal regulations.*

Mohit was aware of this too. In fact his architectural team had disapproved one project in Mumbai for the same reason.

Vishal was saying, *So I have a certain strategy where a big developer or PE fund with deep pocket could execute the project.*

Mr. Mohit was thinking, till now Vishal has put his case in proper prospective with no hidden facts.

But now here comes the crucial point.

'This project is placed about not more than 100 metres from western express highway and near JV link road connecting to central part of Mumbai like Powai, Ghatkopar and Vikhroli. So strategically it is well located with all infrastructure and connectivity in place. According to my company's marketing survey of the region, we have found that there is a huge increase of IT people in last 1 year. This is mainly because NASSCOM has identified this location to boost their sector. So lot of job creation is happening and this may increase in coming years. Of course you could confirm this with your own survey'.

'Interesting' thought Mohit.

'With this potential, 'BHC' can take over this project and be assure of its viability' said Vishal

'But Vishal it is same for all developers and how 'BHC' will benefit differently' asked Mr. Mohit.

'Mohitji the difference is in the project itself' said Vishal.

'How come?' quizzed Mohit finishing his coffee.

'Mohitji as your target market would change from middle class to upper middle class or specifically IT and ITes

audience you could build quality residential and commercial spaces with premium. It is the 'premium touch' which would separate the project from others. And premium would resolve the approval plan issue too because with same built-up area you would have premium pricing. So your profitability will not affect'.

Hmmm.... Mohit was thoughtful.

'How about the existing builder? It would be viable only if he releases at good price for us'.

Vishal said nodding 'Navinbhai, that is the builder, is paid up less than 100 cr and servicing the interest on it. For him it would make sense to sell the project albeit with profit. So what remains would be how much you value against his valuation'.

'Well. It always comes to that, is it not? asked Mr. Mohit smiling, And what you think would be the valuation, Vishal?'

'According to me, premium valuation would not be less than 200cr with back of the envelope calculation. You could of course employ your sources to confirm the valuation. I am not taking the value of the project 3 years from now which would increase at least forty percent. I am being conservative here Mohit'.

'It sound interesting to me Vishal and how much does the builder release it for?'

'My guess is between 120 to 130 cr.'

'Hmm..... this sounds interesting proposal Vishal. No wonder Mr. Mahesh Dubey was keen that I should meet you. I know *the reason now. Vishal, we would be doing due-diligence and then taking the decision. I would visit the site once with my team'* said Mr. Mohit.

'Of course and I would be sending our senior colleague Mr. Ashok Lalka with all relevant documents and technical aspects' concluded Vishal and left.

Mr. Mohit was in thought for long time. Vishal has presented the project nicely. If Vishal says as it is then I do not mind taking the project. I would do all my checks and cross check first. Let me get the details first.

He got the details with Mr. Ashok Lalka after two days.

'This gentleman is so thorough in the paper work. His technical and legal aspects are mind blowing. Alas, he was in my team. He knows the nuisances in Indian regulation so correctly, even my team does not know it' thought Mr. Mohit. He was highly impressed with Mr. Ashok.

Vishal after talking with Ashokbhai thought, now it is a waiting game. They would need 2 weeks time to get a clear picture. But he was surprised to get the call within 10 days from Mr. Ranade. He was praising Mr.Ashok and even commented it is difficult to get people like him nowadays. Vishal smiled. After a week's time meeting took place at 'BHC' office at BKC and the deal was through. He knew Navinbhai would not hang on the project for long and will be relieved by it. So it was a win-win solution for all. Next week Navinbhai called him at his office and released everybody's brokerage even Shirishbhai. He gave the responsibility to Vishal.

'BHC' had liked the project of Guptaji mainly because Navinbhai was very thorough with his paper work and payment part. Navinbhai was happy to transfer all the rights of development to capable company. In fact he was very insistent on it. 'BHC' had liked the project because they have to just put money with no other tedious and ever lasting regulatory work. In fact it was given to them on platter. Navinbhai was happy to hand over the project for 130 crores. Finally they had agreed upon 125 crores after doing their due diligence. It was a cool profit of more than 35 crores for Navinbhai. Vishal had given 'BHC' the valuation of more than 200 crores which turned out to be exact according to their valuation team.

Later Vishal came to know that Navinbhai had bought land parcel of adjacent area, now closed industrial complex. His insistence of good company was to increase the demand of the locality.

Navinbhai knew that company with deep pockets would execute the project.

Vishal thought 'nobody can beat Navinbhai with money'. He admired his shrewd business sense.

Meanwhile Vishal was into his fourth branch after breaking even with the three branches. 'BHC' was very happy with Vishal's work and had recommended him for the Boston conference after hearing his vision for Indian real estate market.

He had to just complete the formality with the 'BHC' today. He had appointment with them at 12.30 pm. He had requested Ashokbhai to come along.

At 2 o clock, everybody was at his house. All old friends; Asifbhai, Ashokbhai, Manoj and even kaka was present.

Diksha had not forgotten him. They all were seated at the dining table and enjoying the gujarathi lunch.

Ashokbhai said, 'Today officially our Guptaji project is done and handed over to 'BHC'. Asifbhai said, 'Yeh bahut achha hua Ashokbhai. Vishal tunne sambhal liya sab kuch. Shirishbhai ka chehara dekhne layak tha voh din Guptaji ke paas. Maine suna hai ki Guptaji uska brokerage nahi denge'.

Ashokbhai said, 'Chodo na Asifbhai. "Kar bhala toh, ho bhala".

Manoj said,' Yeh aap ne sahi kaha.'

Diksha asked, 'Kaka, aap kadi lenge chawal ke sath, ya daal chahiye?' Kaka said, 'Aare, aare nahi, sab kuch hai.

Manoj asked, 'Arey Diksha bhabhi, bag pack ho gaya, Vishalbhai ka?'

Diksha answered, 'Abhi nahi, thodi chize baki hai.'

Manoj said, 'Main kuch madat kar du?'

Diksha said, *"Nahi, nahi, aap sirf rat ko gadi lekar time par aa jaana."*

Kaka asked, "*Vishal bhai, aap jaha ja rahe ho…*"

"*Boston………..Boston ja rahe hai Vishal bhai*", Manoj said.

Kaka said, *"Ha, ha… wahi wahi jaha aap ja rahe ho……Botton…….waha par aap ko Borivali special chai milegi kya?"*

Everybody started laughing loudly.

Kaka thought, why are they laughing again??

_____

Hindi words / dialects meaning

'dadagiri' : Self proclaimed, forceful and boastful leadership.

'bhai' : Brother but commonly addressed to same aged male.

'gujarathi / gujarati' : One of the languages and/or person having his or his ancestral origin in western Indian state 'Gujarat'.

'marwari' : One of the languages and/or person having his or his ancestral origin in district 'Marwar' of western Indian state 'Rajasthan'.

'dalal' : Broker or mediator or facilitator.

'Nathu Khaira': Any ordinary or non-specific person (similar to 'Tom Dick and Harry' in western world)

'paan': Betel leaf traditionally used as digestive herb eaten after meals but consumed at odd timings or throught the day by some people in India.

'Kaka': Paternal uncle but commonly addressed to elderly person.

'khichdi': Mix of all type or selected cereals and rice cooked together.

'chaddi buddy': Childhood friend.

'kholi': A small room or set of rooms often used by lower income group people as home.

BMC: Brihan Mumbai Muncipal Corporation (Bombay or now addressed as Mumbai Muncipal Corporation)

'buzyness': Slang used for business

'mausambi' or 'narangi': orangy or lemony country made alcoholic drink.

'Chawl' : building made up of small one or two rooms as home for lower income group people.

hindi, gujarati and marathi : 'Hindi' is the national language of India, 'gujarati' is language of western Indian state 'Gujarat' and 'marathi' is language of western (south to Gujarat) state 'Maharashtra'.

Soudda: Deal

'khaddus': slang used in hindi language for egoistic and arrogant person

Boora Waqt: Bad phase of life or situation

BHK: 'B' for bedroom, 'H' for hall/living room and 'K' for kitchen.

'UPites': From 'Uttar Pradesh' (one of the northern states of India)

'Biharis': From 'Bihar' (one of the northern states of India)

'lassi': Sweet or salty thick drink made of curd or butter milk.

'khaddus dimagh': Egoistic and arrogant person with brain / intelligence.

'Lakshmi': Hindu goddess representing money.

'Lakshmi puja': Prayer to Hindu goddess Laxmi representing money

'prasad': small offering to be consumed after the prayer to Hindu God.

'haati ka jod': strong joint where elephants (*haati*) also can not break the bond.

'fevicol': Trade name of adhesive made by 'Pidilite' company) commonly used for strong bond / joint in India

"Jaisa customer, vaisa maal": Product just suiting the customer

"Sona khara cchhe ki nahi?": Gujarati proverb to know the product's genuineness symbolizing gold **(Sona)**

Short Stories

Short Story 1

Property deal: Every Indian story

It was a deciding day for Raman, the property consultant, as the deal would make him cross the 'redline' (loss) and be on the 'black' (profit). He had known the seller of the property for long time in the neighbourhood for almost 10 or more years. Mr.Iyer in his late 60s was eager to sell his house in Mumbai's western suburb of Goregaon, Bangur Nagar as he wanted to settle at his native place Kerala with his brother's family. Bangur Nagar was south Indian dominated vicinity with a temple, all cultural & religious programmes held regularly in the neighbourhood. The chances of buyer had to be south Indian as it was the most appropriate locality for them. Raman had given ads in the local hand-outs, newspaper and some other south Indian magazine. He had received a call about a month back. The process had gone smoothly till today when it had culminated into a negotiation meeting to be held in his office at 4 pm in the evening.

He had all the documents ready and spoken to Mr. Iyer about the deal and other relevant factors. Raman had the habit of seeing/visiting before selling any property; that made him assess the property as well as the owner's status. He always had friendly way of doing business, rarely displaying any fenestration of stress or irritation of his personal matter. But today may be little different.

Raman used to do about 4-5 deals in a month regularly of which 3 to 4 were rental and 1 or nothing of outright. He was always on the lookout for outright deals. He used to feel rental deals were good only for commercial premises but not so lucrative for residential. This belief was turning out to be wrong again as his earlier beliefs. He thought how much real estate has taught him and his ideas about life. He had seen extreme people from a well season investor to a desperate seller and their behaviour in this 5 years of consultancy.

Journey of a Broker

Today would decide that the business he started five years back would break even or no? He calculated his biz financial with his old school cum chartered accountant friend, Rakesh. His CA friend had explained him, the finances of big businesses. Raman was curious about the entire thing. He had visited Rakesh's house to know all about it on one of his busy Sundays.

This was about 2 years back and he along with Rakesh had calculated that he is working with a loss or 'redline'. They both had come to conclusion that to be profitable and grow, Raman should be at least have 10% profit (15 was good figure) after expenses to begin with. He was aghast by the calculation and understood all the property businesses in his vicinity and elsewhere (except few) were in the same boat. They manage their expenses; personal and household (few outstation trips included) and were happy and contend.

Raman had decided that he would break the mould and grow with his property consultancy. He did not want to remain in the same vicinity for years and have a death like Mr. Koshi uncle (elderly property agent); but propagate all over the city. He set out the target for his biz with the help of Rakesh who would guide him financially.

So today's deal will set him profitable for this year. One more revelation during these contemplative months was his rental deals were major contributors to the revenue. He had underestimated or had given 'step-motherly' treatment, so as to say, towards it. He saw 80 % of his revenue was from rental deals and consistent. It dawn on him that he was seating on a gold mine. After that, he had focus his energy to uplift the services for rental deals. He started maintaining the record /data and to his surprise the portfolio for rental deals had increased to almost two fold which also started attracting outright deals. Mr. Iyer had come to him this way referred by his neighbour Mr. Subramnayam, a client of Raman for renting out his other residence.

All were seating at Raman's modest office. Mr. Iyer was seating on Raman's chair as it was the most comfortable and reserved for senior most person in the room. The buyer were young couple from Bengaluru with the boy's paternal uncle, Mr.Murthy staying in the neighbourhood who had initiated the process. He had got the young couple Vasudev and Vidya to the neighbourhood who immediately had decided to buy a place here in Bangur Nagar. They both were working in Goregoan east locality in reputed IT companies and traveling would be most favourable from here. They had liked the flat of Mr. Iyer. So they were here for further decisions.

Raman started with all unimportant issues of property, leading gradually to the main issue of budget. Both Vasudev and Vidya were eligible for the loan comprising 80% of the budget amount with 20% amount of the deal manageable by them and their parent's help. Mr. Murthy was well aware of this but insisted on reducing the price of the 2 BHK flat. He was harping on the price to be more than the market price by the recently concluded deal of adjacent society of same configuration (2 BHK) to almost 1.24 crores. Mr. Iyer was expecting 1.40 crores and had reduced the price to 1.34 crores on Raman;s insistence of valuation. The value of 1.34 crores was not acceptable by Mr. Murthy. There was lot of discussion on the amount and finally it had come to deadlock by Mr. Murthy insistence on 1.25 crores as final offer and Mr. Iyer not refusing below 1.34 crores.

As Raman was broker for both the sides he had to maintain the balance. But here he thought the market price of flat in the adjacent society was not to be compared as it was an old society and there were talks on redevelopment too. So the price of Mr. Iyer was decent enough for the deal. He knew Mr.Murthy is trying 'take or leave it' tactic with Mr. Iyer. He knew Mr. Iyer to be simple person and had done very few or negligible property dealings in his life. According to the market and state of property 1.34 crores was decent enough offer. He knew Mr.Murthy is trying out evasive technique with

Mr. Iyer. Mr. Iyer being naïve in this kind of dealings turned his face towards Raman with resigned look. Raman thought it was the time for him to take side with Mr. Iyer as the deal offered by him was genuine enough. Raman knew that Vasudev and Vidya had loved the flat and society. Mr. Subrmanyam the neighbour of the flat had invited them to his place with Mrs. Subrmanyam insisted on offering filter coffee (a staple beverage of south Indians) during one of the site visits. They had discussed everything about the family and native place. Vidya had liked Subrmanyam aunty and would be very happy to shift there. Raman knew all this and knew he had to give emotional reason to the couple but logical reason to Mr. Murthy.

So being mute spectator for almost 15 minutes he turned towards Vasudev and Vidya and said it would be great loss for them to lose a flat of Mr. Iyer as the flat had seen progress of Mr. Iyer family. He had started as assistant manager and retired as vice president in a reputed company. He would have afforded to shift at some good place in town side like Matunga inhabited with south Indians. (Vidya & Vasudev had visited that place to meet Vidya's maternal aunty when they had shifted newly and were thinking of buying the place there, but after knowing the budget had abandon the idea). Raman was continuing that Mr. Iyer's son had settled down in the US and was inviting his parents for good. But Mr. Iyer like old people wanted to be near his roots at the evening of his life and had refused. His daughter had settled down in Australia and doing well. So this property was a good omen for its inhabitants. Now too, his son had insisted on not selling the flat but Mr. Iyer had refused to take any money from his son and wanted to settle with his wife in Kerala along his brothers with his own money. With some of his savings and extra money from the property sale he would leave a modest retired life. Mr. Iyer had insisted to sell this flat to decent family and would wait for the right time.

Raman gave a deliberate pause and smile to the couple. He knew in their eyes that he had sold the flat to the couple emotionally.

He now turned towards the tough task; Mr. Murthy.

He said, Mr. Murthy the flat you are talking is in the old society and may go for redevelopment. That flat had come to me for sale but did not show you as I knew you would never agree to it as the staying would be a problem in immediate future. That kind of flats are meant for investment and not for staying and I would not give even 1.20 crores to it. The property is good for investment and should not fetch more than 1.10 crores according to my calculation if it has to give me good returns. Forget all this Mr. Murthy, tell me you are staying in flat worth how much?

Mr. Murthy said, almost 1.45 to 1.5 crores as it has more carpet area comprising one extra puja room.

And what price you bought for?

Mr. Murthy after thinking said, I think I bought for 50 lakhs some 10 years back.

Raman said, so now the property has appreciated about 2 and half times than the buying price in 10 years. So if you would have bought the property for say 48 or 52 lakhs 10 years back, had it made in difference now after 10 years? What is 2 lakhs in 10 years' time for your property? Same way what is 9 lakhs (difference) for this property given in good faith and goodwill to these wonderful young couple who may stay at least for coming 10 years. See for the long term Mr. Murthy. I think the offer by Mr. Iyer is fair enough and I agree with it. It is okay even if I lose a deal because I think the cost of the property is very less as compare to price offered.

What do you mean by cost less than price? asked Mr. Murthy and Vasudev together.

Raman said, you hardly have to do any major work as all the structural & civil work was completed by Mr. Iyer by insistence of his son visiting last time. You only need to paint the house and get furniture to your taste. He has done all work using good quality material (you may ask Mr. Subrmanayam), so any major repair work for coming 10 -15 years is out of question. If you deduct this cost you are for profit and not loss in this deal. And also Mr. Iyer said to me that Vidya reminded him of his daughter.

Vidya looked at Mr. Iyer with warm eyes and Vasudev towards Mr. Murthy with questioning eyes.

There was a silence at this moment and with experience Raman had known not to say anything for some time. He indicated the same by putting his palm on Mr Iyer's hidden lap under the table.

After lot of exchanges among the Murthys and with his typical expressionless face Mr. Murthy said that he will convey the decision late in the evening.

Raman said, till when should I expect the decision? as he need to look for other buyers?

Vasudev said instinctively, he would convey the decision in two hours, which is by 7 pm.

Raman said he would wait till 8 pm.

After all had left (with sad Mr. Iyer), Raman knew the deal is almost done but Mr. Murthy is a tough candidate to negotiate? He wonder what is his profession.

The call did not come that evening nor in the night.

Raman said to Mr. Iyer on the phone that we will wait till tomorrow evening 7 pm and not be in haste to call them. Mr. Iyer reluctantly agreed.

Next day morning he received a call from Vasudev saying he would like to come and meet him. Raman said to come by 9.30 am to his office. Mr. Vasudev and VIdya were there at his office and refused any beverages offered by Raman.

Vasudev said, they would like to go ahead with the deal. I have got a cheque of 2 lakhs as token to offer Iyer uncle.

Raman said, where is Mr. Murthy?

Vasudev said, we have spoken with him.

Raman said, it would be better if Mr. Murthy be present at such moment.
Vasudev and Vidya exchanged glances.
Vasudev said, Murthy uncle thinks we would get a better offer from Mr. Iyer if we wait. But we do not like to wait.
Vidya was looking down searching for some hidden point.
Raman said, I still insists that you get Mr. Murthy along and I am sure Mr. Iyer would also like it that way.
Vasudev said, but we have decided for the flat come what-so-ever.
Raman said, I know but it is always better to get your elder's blessing before embarking on any new venture.
Vidya said holding Vasudev's hand, okay Raman anna (elder brother), we would get Murthy uncle in the evening.
In the evening, all were present at the meeting.
Raman said softy, Murthy sir I think you are getting a fair deal.
Mr. Murhty said, I know Raman, I found about it with other brokers and some known people. I think you are close enough with your estimate and I have told them (looking at the Vasudev & Vidya) to go ahead. But they insisted that I hand over the token money to Mr. Iyer. So here Mr. Iyer sir, here is the token of 2 lakhs (handing over the cheque towards Mr. Iyer).
Mr Iyer said, thank you.
Vasudev said, I would need copies of the property for the processing of loan.
Raman said, everything is ready and in place.
Raman could not hide a smile thinking ; here is a young couple looking for beginning of their journey, middle aged person guiding them and an elderly person planning for retirement. What a typical Indian real estate story.
And the deal was closed in 2 months' time.

Journey of a Broker

Short Story 2

Wisdom in real estate investment

One of my neighbour's father, an old man in seventies (fit & fine) met me while departing for work. The talks ended up with real estate market scenario.
He said he has 4-5 properties (3 of them prime, 1 is at outskirts of Mumbai & in 1 he is residing) which gives him more than 1L or so monthly in today's scenario.
I said, You invested prudently.
He said, 'Yes what appears prudent was not so 10 years back. I was opposed by my son (your friend). He had advised me to invest in stocks but i said i do not understand stocks. I am comfortable in real estate. I have seen it and understand it. But I have also been ditched by it couple of times'.
I was interested. You rarely hear failures in this boastful world of success. I probed him further and he was willing to open up but at the cost of 'kadak chai' (strong flavour tea). I was overwhelmed by his 'down to earth' and 'matter-of-fact attitude'.
After some time he was revealing his cookies over his 'masala chai' and i was dunking on his wisdom. He was saying, i am not educated like you all people but understand 'dhanda' very well. I have been doing garment manufacturing for years but now retired. I was able to marry off my sisters, separate from my brothers and set a sound business for my two sons. They are all well settled now. I retired 5 years back from business but never from investing as it is never ends.
I asked him, how it is so?
He said i never got enough money from biz as i thought i would, but it only took care of everyday chores and family duties. Most of us never earn; atleast I, could never earn from biz as these big corporate houses. I understood my limitation late in life but realized that the place which i owned has appreciated several times over. Everybody realizes this but

few understand the meaning behind it. It takes time for a place to appreciate irrespective of economy of the country. As we are placed in Mumbai it has to grow, being a financial capital. The only difference he said (i was keenly listening to his secret) is micro-market location and timing to exit.
Can you please elaborate kaka (uncle)?
'Location comes with aptitude (sense of market dynamics) but timing comes up with patience. You need to hold it till the right moment or time'.
I asked, you mean we should time the market?
He emphatically said 'No, but 'time' yourself.
I said, i did not understand.
'Sometimes you sell a property because you are getting more returns but investing in the next investment spoils the whole purpose. You should be ready or have next investment worked out in mind in case you sell this existing real estate'.
'And it should give returns more than the existing one' I said thoughtfully absorbing this common sense yet rare attribute. After a pause i asked in affirmative tone, you lost money this way couple of times?
'Now you understood', he said finishing off his chai.

Short Story 3

Smile @ Architect

Navinchand Gopichand Kamra a.k.a. Navinbhai, the builder to real estate fraternity was approaching towards his office building with deliberate and purposeful steps. He had done this few times in last 15 – 16 years for his property development business.

Today was one of the important days of his life but he was relatively calm about it. He had faced this kind of anxiety several times before yet he had realized that he could be calm on these occasions. In fact, one of his long-time colleague cum accountant Sharmaji had also mentioned about his detachment attitude during these stressful moments. Navinbhai did not know how he acquired this coolness but he had decided long ago that when he would not be able to handle this moments or pressure points in life, he would retire.

But today was different; he knew the answer to his coolness but he was not able to place it correctly. He thought it was a defining moment for him personally and to the real estate sector to some extent. Nobody was aware of his decision except his long-time friend and business associate cum investor Mr. I M Parekh. Parekhbhai as he was known among his friends was a seasoned investor and had known Navinbhai for almost more than 15 years. He was the first person to believe in Navinbhai and invested in him and not his project. Parekhbhai knew that Navinbhai was right and sensible in his approach and never proven otherwise till now. Mr. I M Parekh was aware that Navinbhai does not call him to the office except for some major decision. He may be needing him for advice, investment or outside point of view which was Parekhbhai's favourite aspect. He gave insight to Navinbhai in different perspective but when he reflected on such meetings he thought he has learned so much from Navinbhai rather than other way.

So here was Navinbhai sitting on his desk while his team was gathering around this worn out conference table, witness to so many decisions, arguments, celebrations and people. He knew he was perceived as neutral entity in real estate sector among the big players. In fact he was approached so many times to resolve the issues among the builders/developers' lobby and was successful most of the time. Navinbhai was lowly placed in the highest league of developers but that was mainly because of his morally tilted side. He believed the every biz should generate profits but not profits over profits as was the case of few crony developers.

Today was a significant day and he knew he was going to ruffle few nay many feathers in the industry.

Navinbhai was viewing his accountant Sharmaji a staunch loyalist taking a seat near him. While Sharmaji was uttering something, Navinbhai with subconscious nodding was looking at their architect Mr Govind Rao for 15 years; from an old school and revealing no features as usual on his face. Rao saheb, as he was called by everybody, was accompanied with a new architect Ms. Shreya Rathi who was affectionately groomed by him. She was turning out to be right choice by Rao saheb's mentoring. Navinbhai knew the happiest person in today's meeting would be Rao saheb.

He saw his marketing team getting assembled and taking their seat as well as the legal team. The marketing & sales team's head Kishore was in his jolly mood (always) and passing some insignificant remarks to lighten the mood around the table. Navinbhai even noticed Chandru, the peon placing water bottles and tea in front of the Mr. Rao, a tea addict. Mr I. M Parekh was sitting in the corner of the room drinking coffee watching out of the window facing the parking lot.

Navinbhai started with no customary greetings but to the point 'Marketing the new project' agenda. He asked Rao saheb about the details of the new project they were about to launched. Rao saheb in his customary 'no nonsense' voice was dabbling out the details which in brief was; 10 million square feet of residential area to be built in first phase followed by 5 million square feet in second phase and then 2.5 million luxurious and 2.5 million square feet commercial units in last and third phase about 5-7 years from now. Total 20 million square feet project in 7 years to be build, situated about 500 meters off the main LBS Marg, a busy arterial road on Eastern suburbs of Mumbai populated with Maharashtrians.

He asked Sharmaji the finance guy and Sharmaji in his inept (out of place) style and heavy 'Hindi' accent launched with his figures. In brief Sharmaji was telling that the project was about to cost INR 200 – 250 crores and about INR 80 – 100 crores with servicing the interest, it would go to more than INR 350 crores project.

Selling the project 'per se' was not the issue as the location was favourable but the demand was less because of recent policies by the NaMo government in the form of RERA, GST, Benami Act and demonetization. The reduction in home loan rates was not helping the sentiment.

Navinbhai knew there has to be new or different strategy. He asked the marketing head Kishore whether he has any unique marketing strategy but not completely satisfied with Kishore's idea of labeling the project as 'New Girgaum or New Shivaji Park' as it would attract Maharashtrian population in general and give them the satisfaction of shifting their old roots rather than leaving their roots altogether.

Navinbhai like the idea but it needed refining as this strategy was used earlier with other developers. He thought we could use this strategy along with the measures I am about to announced. So grossly he approved Kishore's strategy but with refining it further.

Ultimately it would boiled down to the cost and demand in the market. Navinbhai paused with the hand held in air to denote silence. All knew something drastic was going to be announced. Everybody was 'all ears' now.

Navinbhai said, it is for the first time I would be taking this decision which may prove wrong but I will take the risk at the expense of long term vision of this organization. I am being serving this industry for more than 20 years as a developer and sadly (and embarrassed) to have been brought to notice about the state of the sector by the competent pro-people government that, "the customer" is ultimately the decision maker of any sector. The policies announced by the government is 'reading on the wall' in capital letter to be seen by real estate sector. I hereby declared that I will be selling all my future projects in carpet area rates only. You may say that everybody mentions the carpet area (as we do too) but sell the property in super built-up parameters. We would from now on be selling the project in carpet area rates & nothing else and that too at the most reasonable cost with no dilution to the quality of our construction and services. We charge about 40-100 % premium over carpet area but form now onward it would not be more than 15 % as we know the built-up area is never above that margin. All super built-up calculation will go away. We will be building super built-up area, common maintenance or other facilities as our service to the customers. I know I may ruffle lot of feathers in the industry but I am ready for the grind.

Navinbhai saw towards Rao saheb who was smiling form ears to ears but all others were dead silent.

Navinbhai continued, I am aware that many of you may thinking that I am not being an astute business man.

Sharmaji said reactively, yes Navinbhai; we would face no or very minor profit & with this much investment, we need to have much better margins.

Navinbhai continued as if Sharmaji had not spoken, "with this step I want to redefine real estate sector as customer friendly, at least I would like to position myself as that."

He recognized the marketing head nodding his head emphatically.

He continued; imagine the brand we would be creating in the market. This project may not give us the profit for now but it would allow us a platform or foundation of our future new projects. And I assure you that I would not be bogged down by crony players of the field. I also assure that you would be working for the best organized company in future. I reassure all the stakeholders, employees, vendors and other associates to believe in me and my vision.

With the end of the speech he looked towards Mr. I M Parekh who was showing appreciation and joining the applause with others in the room.

Even Chandru was clapping along with others without understanding the intricacies of the matter.

Navinbhai looking at Rao saheb could not help thinking that this must be the first time after a very long time (actually after graduation) that Rao saheb was genuinely happy and smiling shamefully; with Shreya in tears consoling him.

Short Story 4

Tale of Mumbai's Real Estate investor

Sandeep was MNC employee staying in upper middle class locality with a deluxe car, house, bank balance and enviable family. But he had a different approach towards wealth and believed that wealth should belong to people who are professionals and educated. He himself was an IIT & an IIM product with huge potential. He used to always argue with his father about the wealth creating people as against wealth stagnating and non-growing people. His father himself an IIT person never went for money as was the case with lot of old generation and used to be 'quite' in these conversations. He used to always smile at Sandeep when he was asked why his father did not earn money when he could have easily done it. Sandeep's day would begin by commuting to his office around 8.30 am. On his way out of society complex, his car would stop to join the main lane of the vicinity and exactly at this juncture were row of nine shops. Of the lot, the prime shop belong to real estate consultant named 'Sweet Home Property'. It belong to Mr. Dharmesh Raja called by everybody as Dharmeshbhai. Sandeep used to pass the shop without paying much attention. Only thing which registered with him was the name 'Sweet Home Property'. Whenever he talked about property market with his colleagues or friends, this name used to appear unconsciously, may be because of seeing the board for last 5 years regularly in the morning and evening.

He was contemplating of investing in the property as he had some fund lying with him and after discussing about the investment, had come to conclusion of buying real estate. He thought of finding the scenario in real estate market.

So subsequent Sunday he went to meet Dharmeshbhai. Dharmeshbhai's office was a 'well-to-do' office without any frills. It had decent décor and adequate furnishing with a

warm ambience. Once you go to 'Sweet Home Property' office you tend to like it. You may not know the exact reason or put a finger for liking but the overall effect was warmth and welcoming. Like his office décor, Dharmeshbhai was a warm person almost the same age of Sandeep. He had a heavy Guajarati accent with passable spoken English.
They introduced each other.
Sandeep was seated comfortably in the chair eyeing the office and its content.
'Not bad' for a real estate agent, Sandeep's track of thoughts had started.
Dharmeshbhai was observing Sandeep and not interrupting Sandeep's thought. He was used to this first reaction of customers and had over a period of time known not to stop it. He knew about the effect of his space on customers and allowed it to sink in. He hardly lost any genuine customers and few whom he lost turned to be his best friends.
'He must be doing very well for a property agent. So nice to be wealthy without doing any hard work. May be he must have hit some few lucky deals.....on & on', Sandeep thoughts were running.
After touring the imaginary success journey of realtor, Sandeep returns his gaze to smiling Dharmeshbhai.
Dharmeshbhai, how is the market for buying real estate? asked Sandeep.
Sandeepbhai, it depends on the purpose you want to buy for; but overall it is buyer's market, replied Dharmeshbhai keeping coffee in front, which his helper Magan had got.
I am thinking of buying my second house, said Sandeep with a pinch of pride and the hot disposable coffee glass.
Dharmeshbhai nodded his head with a smile.
Sandeep believing encouraged said, I am thinking of creating some asset for myself. I already do some investment in mutual funds since last 5 years and I have a decent amount with me.
What is your budget Sandeepbhai?

Say about 60 to 70 lakhs, came the reply.
And how much would be the loan and how much equity?
I have about 30 lakhs and am eligible for another 40 lakhs loan.
You must be paying some loan if I may ask, for your present house?
Yes, about 75K for a loan of 90 lakhs and never missed my instalment. It would get over in 3 years' time.
Good, good. So we would consider our budget to be somewhere between 65-70 lakhs and additional EMI of 35-40 K, right?
Yes somewhere around that.
Do you have any liking or biased for residential property like 1, 2 or 3 BHKs?
I am open to options.
Dharmeshbhai was writing all the information into a form of about 3 pages. He asked Sandeep all property related questions.
Sandeep was surprised by this interaction as he always thought the agents do not do this kind of things with anyone. So he asked reluctantly, Dharmeshbhai why are you taking this kind of information?
Dharmeshbhai said, I am trying to understand your requirement and needs properly before I begin my search for your property.
Oh… but no brokers does this….
Yes very few of us do this and we also maintain records of the deals.
That is very impressive Dharmeshbhai.
Oh, thank you!
Sandeepbhai, let me go through requirements and get back to you in two days. But I would like to know why are you buying this property?
Sandeep surprisingly said, 'why meaning? As I said I need to create asset'.
That means you want to invest or would like to stay there?

No I am happy with my residence. I would like to invest in it. Ok… now I got it.
Sandeep said, Ok then let me know in 2 days' time.
Sandeep received expected call from Dharmeshbhai exactly in 2 days and asking for few more days. It was decided to meet after a week.
Dharmeshbhai was waiting for Sandeep.
He was made comfortable with hot coffee glass and cool temperature soothing his nerves collected from the office.
Dharmeshbhai said without wasting time looking at the paper in his hand, 'Sandeepbhai I would suggest 4 options to you'.
Dharmeshbhai went on, One is buying a 2 BHK ready possession flat at Mira road which would cost about 55 – 60 lakhs or so; second is 1 BHK ready possession at LBS Marg Bhandup / Nahur vicinity costing about 55 – 60 lakhs and third under construction property of 2 BHK at Borivali west costing 90 lakhs as of now to be paid slab wise till 3 years.
He had all the details typed neatly on an A4 paper.
Sandeep was thoroughly impressed.
Sandeep asked, what is the 4th option Dharmeshbhai?
Dharmeshbhai said, fourth option is one small shop in our vicinity of Powai.
Dharmeshbhai waited for the information to be absorbed by Sandeep.
Sandeep said, 'Mira road & Borivali are too far; Bhandup I can think of but shop I do not think will work for me. I will not be able handle the tenants of the shop'.
Dharmeshbhai said, let me explain Sandeepbhai, let us take all the options one by one.
Since our budget is 60 lakhs I suggested different configurations at four different locations, right?
Right…
Now these three locations have got all relevant physical and social infrastructure and lot of new real estate activity happening around it.
But Dharmeshbhai, I do not want to go there.

I know Sandeepbhai, but let me finish. So these two localities (Mira Road & Borivali) are good for appreciation point of view. That means you may get returns of 20- 25 % in 5 years duration because they are strategically placed.
The percentage had alerted Sandeep.
If the proposed flyover and metro is done then the appreciation may go up further if we move in early.
Dharmeshbhai but I would not buy there any time as it is too far.
Sandeepbhai, you are creating wealth right?
Yeessss!
Then why are you sticking to the vehicle? See the goal.
Meaning?
Sandeepbhai, I am not telling you to buy and expect you to stay there. That, I am well aware. I am telling you that, we will treat them like vehicles to get us towards our goal and that is maximum returns. 20 – 25 % is good returns for real estate investment. In 4 years it would appreciate at least 60-70 % or above 1 crore in price.
How much do you guarantee it Dharmeshbhai?
I do not guarantee anything, I am just providing options for us to see all the possibilities. For real estate to appreciate it takes at least 5 years; not evenly through the years but you do see some spikes and some ditches but the overall effect is 20 % in 5 – 7 years if chosen properly. It may vary from location to location and property to property & also your timing of buying at the spike or selling at the worst ditch. You may go wrong some time but the risks are neutralized by choosing various parameters responsible for growth of property and understanding the market. Hence what I am providing is thought-out and researched options.
You mean Dharmeshbhai, you have researched these properties.
Absolutely Sandeepbhai, I had been to lot of places and shortlisted these 4 options.
Oookkk....

So considering the possibility of only appreciation for investment and not end-use, we should look at these options too.
The third options is Bhandup with same criteria.
What about the fourth option Dharmeshbhai? asked curious Sandeep.
The shop would give your monthly rent taking care of your EMI to some extent. And the shop appreciation in our vicinity is definitely good as you may have guessed.
But managing the tenants is not my cup of tea, Dharmeshbhai.
For that i am there if you have faith in me.
Ohhh.... But something does not work out between us then..
You are free to go to anyone Sandeepbhai & I will see to it that you get the right person.
But you may lose business Dharmeshbhai.
But relationship are important Sandeepbhai. If we have cordial relationship then you may do future business with me. So I may not lose business actually, said Dharmeshbhai with his trademark warm smile.
Of course Dharmeshbhai.
And you are free to walk away anytime from me.
Sandeep was thinking, this Dharmeshbhai is different from other brokers I have encountered.
Ok Dharmeshbhai, I will let you know in few days.
Of course, Sandeepbhai, please take your time.
Thank you Dharmeshbhai for your advice. How much should I pay for your consultation?
Aarey Sandeepbhai, please do not bother about it and thanks of thinking about me.
But you took effort for my need?
That is alright and I too have acquired information. So please do not bother about it at all. And also please convey my thanks to your father for referring me the customer.
Sandeep was perplexed.
What customer?

One young man, Hari from your native place who has shifted to Mumbai recently. Your father had got him and his friends as they were looking for 2 BHK flat on rent to share. They would shift in 2 days.

Ohh... really, I was not aware of it?

Aarey your father is a great man Sandeepbhai. Hari was telling me that he has helped so many young students from your native place settling down in metro cities for jobs and stays. He is a great man. Hari was praising him endlessly. I am lucky to be associated with him in any way I could.

Sandeep was in daze returning home. He now understood his father's frequent visits to their native place and silence in their conversations.

Today he was amazed two fold by the customer centric approach of Dharmeshbhai and magnanimous nature of his misunderstood father.

He realized he was wrong about so many assumptions. His respect for both these person increased tremendously.

After 2 months, Sandeep invested in Borivali west property suggested by Dharmesbhai.

Journey of a Broker

Short Story 5

Investment; the ultimate ecstasy...

This is a story influenced by one of my investor friends (huge investments in real estate) who is perceived as money minded. But after knowing him closely, I have begun to understand his philosophy towards life. He says everyone has different attributes and I may be good at money. So I am using my financial aptitude for betterment of society which is not perceived by society at large. I do not want to prove anybody anything but myself and am at peace with myself. I did not understand his angle initially but have started appreciating his point of view over a period of almost 15 years. This story is with reference to many such investors......

What would give us ultimate happiness? One disciple asked Buddha. He smiled and said with a purposeful pause, "That is for you to find out."

The disciple did not understand the answer first but later during his sessions with Buddha started discovering it.

Well what is it that makes you happy? One investor was asked and he answered "Making money'.

All reporters and journalists defamed him and used all materialistic proofs to make him an anti-poor, anti-social figure. NGOs vowed not to take his charity and he was malafide in all possible ways.

He on the other hand was completely cool. He did not speak to any social bodies, organization or others who were anti capitalists for some time. He went on doing what he loved. After few years one of his friends asked him what he would do with all the money.

He smiled and said with a purposeful pause "that is for you to find out".

And indeed the friend found out about him with all the access available and proximity to the investor.

After few months it so happened that both friends were called for the same seminar on investments. The investor's friend was asked to conclude the seminar.
This is what he said,
"Friends, here we have come together to know ways of making more and more money. Everyone wants to know about it through the legends sitting out here on dais. And as you may know by now that no one has said what you want to hear and that my friends, is the key to the answer of making money.
Money is not made for the sake of it but it is the bye product of what we actually are doing. We ignore the deeds of the successful investors because of our 'moneyed' glasses miss to grasp the art of making money. These investors have realized that going after money is not the right way but sharing knowledge, teaching or helping others is the right way. Is it not paradoxical? I too thought the same. But believe me it is not. Saraswati (goddess of knowledge) would get Laxmi (goddess of wealth) and not the other way.
Some of you may be working, some doing business or self-employed. The person who believes in you is the person who has faith in you or sees some positive spark in you. An employer may see that loyalty and integral individual in you, clients seeing well intended efforts by a self-employed consultant, a financer a robust cash positive model in your business and so on. It is the investor in that employer, client and financer who sees the return on the investment he is making on you. This may be intangible for lot of us but for few rare ones, it is tangible and seen with clarity. There is one more thing that I would like to point out with this investor clan and it is the happiness they get when they see employees, self-employed or businesses flourish as you know **there is no big happiness than the happiness you give others**. There are investors who invest for self-happiness, self-indulgence but there are rare investors who invest to make the society a better place by promoting talent, identifying entrepreneurs

closing gaps in insufficient services and products in society, taking businesses to the next level and making the world a better place to live. Friends, we have one such person amongst us today and I would like you to reintroduce him…"
The speaker turned around towards the investor friend but saw an empty chair…
The investor friend had left the seminar few moments back to continue his work of making money.

Short Story 6

Brokerage at stake!

The scene was Umeshbhai's office at the prime location of Andheri West; western suburbs of Mumbai. There was an argument between Umeshbhai & Santoshbhai two prominent property brokers in the vicinity. Both had known each other for more than 15 years and been close friends despite being professional rivals for the same period. In fact both had supported each other during their respective bad phases which made them come closer. Their families exchange greetings, gifts and shared miseries on many occasions. Both friends were loud and had differences in their brokerage consultancies which was always a talking point and showcase for many other peers.

Today the topic was renewal of brokerage of rental properties. The person responsible was Karan, a small time broker in the vicinity. He was not being paid by the buyer as well as the seller for the renewal of rental agreement. Both had denied him payment on the basis that they need no broker to renew the agreement and it was a mutual understanding among them.

Karan had called Santoshbhai as he knew him through one deal done few months earlier. Also Santoshbhai was a treasurer and committee member of the broker's association in the vicinity. Santoshbhai had similar problem in the past and put up this issue in front of the committee with no solution but only debate and more debate. After hearing Karan's issue, Santoshbhai's dormant problem has been activated and reaching its crescendo. He had immediately called Umeshbhai who then suggested to meet at his office. Umeshbhai was secretary of the association for the last 5 years and dealt with many issues of brokers with fairly good result.

Santoshbhai was almost shouting at Umeshbhai implying the issue has become very common and prevalent in the vicinity and something has to be done about it. Umeshbhai knowing Santoshbhai very well, was listening with a grave face and not saying anything at all. He occasionally looked at Karan for approval of the context.

After some repeat commentary from Santoshbhai, Umeshbhai had now drifted to his own thoughts; 'we had discussed this issue and explained Santoshbhai so many times. But Santoshbhai insisted on confronting the seller and buyer and getting paid. Umeshbhai had sought legal opinion on it and discussed this issue with many brokers, committee members and other association. It was prevalent only in some vicinities like theirs and not an issue in another localities. Umeshbhai knew this was not entirely true as lot of brokers do not report this issues to anybody. Umeshbhai has also face this issue and eventually had come to conclusion of resolving it.'

"...... so Umeshbhai I think we should take this matter seriously and get legal sanctioned from the government body."

Umeshbhai waked from his day dreaming just in time for anybody to notice. He now faced his colleagues with few more committee members (invited by Santoshbhai) eagerly waiting for response.

Umeshbhai said, Santoshbhai, I had discussed this issue of brokerage of rental renewal with lot of colleagues in our and other localities. In fact I had taken legal opinion on it. Yes we had to take this matter to government body like RERA (Real Estate Regulation & Development Act) which would take its time. Although you may also approach with this same issue to RERA as individual agent according to their rules. Meanwhile if you are patient enough to hear me out I would suggest some factors to resolve it not entirely but to considerable effect.

Of course, we would hear your views Umeshbhai, said one of the attendees.
Thank you.
Coming to the point directly, Umeshbhai said, See, have we consider why people do not pay brokerage after the renewing the rental agreement?
Somebody said, 'they think we do not deserve it'.
'But we have found the right place for tenant and made the seller and the tenant meet in the first place. We are asking for our renewal fees. This also happens in the bigger commercial & residential deals. So why should we give away our share?' said Karan emphatically.
Yes, yes… affirmative echoes from all other present.
But Karan that is the issue and we are discussing same here; and i am asking again why is that the owners or tenants do not pay us the deserved amount?
Santoshbhai said, 'because they want to save as much as possible.'
'Right, said Umeshbhai 'and we are the easy target'.
Yes you are right Umeshbhai, they think they can get away with it.'
But why are we the easy target or the first liability of any disputed deals. Have you thought of it? asked Umeshbhai in loud and clear voice.
Nobody was answering.
After few seconds Santoshbhai said now cooling down a bit, what do you think Umeshbhai?
Yes, yes Umeshbhai what do you think? Others joined in.
I think we lack communication with them or lack of 'expected services' from their point of view.
How is that Umeshbhai? asked Santoshbhai warming up to the topic.
See if you have good relationship with the seller and we give him good business of rental income regularly, then the seller would not consider of bypassing us. He knows that this

broker would get me tenants if I pay him regularly may be less but pay him...

Are you with me till now? Umeshbhai was asking looking into everyone's eyes.

Most were nodding.

So why would he cut you from the deal if he thinks long term. Because sooner or later he may also sell his property and that you would be his only hope of fetching right price for it. So I think they behave this way for two reasons, said Umeshbhai.

And they are? asked Santoshbhai.

These are; either they are short term thinkers, only thinking about the present scene unable to understand long term benefit out of us.

'And the second one, Umeshbhai' asked Karan eagerly.

Second one Karan, I think we are responsible for it.

How?

They perceive us as non-professionals and our lack of maintaining the relationship with them.

Can you elaborate Umeshbhai?

'How many of you go to the seller or tenants to know /inquire about the status midway during the rental period? We only go when it is time to renew the contract'.

Nobody was answering and few were looking down.

We are not bother about them after we get our brokerage. If we just asked them twice in a year about any issue regarding the property, it would make a huge difference. In fact I am thinking of engaging a property management services to provide maintenance all the time of the year. It would give professional touch and actually help seller in maintaining the property and may be fetch good value for it. Also not to mention additional fees for us. You may also have the same tenant coming to you for further requirement of rent and eventually buying as he would get use to the locality. You may come out with your own ways (and there are many ways) of improving the relationship with them and I think that should resolve the issue to large extend.

But what do I do with this issue? asked Karan dejectedly.

If I were you, I would let it go and learn from it. I know you may lose some money now but would remember it as fees to improve/learn on relationship with the customer. Let us for few moment in all deals, think from their point of view. It would improve not only their life but also our image in the society which is badly needed now in this RERA times.

Yes, yes, you are right Umeshbhai… said everybody together.

Umeshbhai was continuing, I was talking to somebody the other day and he mentioned some property consultant in Andheri East, already doing it for last 10 years. In fact I will be meeting him in a day or two. Anybody is interested in meeting him?

Almost everybody raised their hands including Karan and Santoshbhai.

Short Story 7

Black Pearl in turbulent real estate ocean

Vishal's perennial thought was 'how do I succeed in this cut throat real estate industry?'
He knew everybody had this question one time or another in their professional life, only nobody shares it. Everyone has a hidden agenda here. He too; but he could not help it as he was surrounded by wolves and if he doesn't behave like one, he would be eaten up. This jungle is not for fickle minded sheep.
Vishal was freelance property consultant practicing for more than 5 years in western suburbs of Mumbai. Everybody were biz minded and always looking for "what is in it for me?" attitude. Everyone is a friend and rival at the same time.
Vishal always had this issue (all must be having it!) and needed a friend or mentor who would understand his predicament. He was used to lot of deals and brokers in his profession where he always was looking for such mentor figure. His eyes used to search for such person relentlessly. He never thought he would be meeting such a person, in such an ordinary way.
One day, he was sitting with his nearby property consultant Mr. Pradeep (Pradeepbhai called by everyone) for a 'Leave & License' deal. This was for the shop which Vishal had the keys and was sole dealer, as it belong to an NRI person who had shown trust in him. Vishal on his part had kept the bargain and kept all the transactions transparent.
Pradeepbhai on the other hand was famous for providing short stick of the deal to everyone he encounter.
Pradeepbhai was saying, Vishalbhai, this is
Manohar *kaka* from adjacent locality and is in this property biz since more than 25 years. He is very quiet fellow and keeps to himself. Everybody calls him Manukaka.
Manukaka gave a warm smile to Vishal.

Vishal return the smile with equal fervor and hand shake. Vishal instantly felt relieved of some burden from his mind. He could not fathom his feelings properly but felt very secured and happy in presence of Manukaka.

Manukaka gave a deliberate nod to Vishal as if he knew what Vishal was feeling.

The feeling faded faster than it had come. In fact Vishal would have forgotten about it but he felt the same thing when he met Manukaka later.

The dealing went off smoothly but with little hitch where Pradeepbhai plan to give lesser share to Manukaka.

Manukaka on his part told Pradeepbhai in his soft voice, Pradeepbhai I have earned my living through this sector and am an old timer. Even if you do not pay me I would not be affected. I have earned enough to survive my old age. The money may help you increase your biz. So keep it and pay me if you are willing and in comfortable position.

Pradeepbhai immediately gave the share of brokerage to Manukaka with irrelevant excuses and the deal was closed.

Vishal was impressed and started thinking; what a way to handle things?

If I would be in his position, I would also do it, but alas...

You too could do it Vishalbhai, came the voice of Manukaka outside Pradeepbhai's office.

Vishal was stunned by the statement and was about to ask him how he knew what he was thinking, but decided against it.

Manukaka came to him and said, be yourself and you would excel in your field.

Vishal's eyes met with Manukaka's and had the same feeling of security and peace again.

He could not tolerate this and was about to ask Manukaka after opening his eyes.

Manukaka had departed without any trace.

Vishal thought of the experience for the whole evening and night.

This Manukaka, small framed, dark skin old timer Gujarati was hardly seen by anyone in the crowd. Vishal had seen him so many times later but hardly anyone took any notice of him. He was always warm with everyone and spoke only when spoken to. He was very gentle compare to all other brokers. He was noticed only when you meet him at some dealing or personally.

Vishal was intrigued and wanted to know more about the person. So he started investigating by asking lot of realtors about him. Some people who knew Manukaka would say as Pradeepbhai that he was a gentle person and keeps to himself. Few of them did not recognize the existence of such a person at all.

Vishal had found that Manukaka's office was about 10 minutes form his place. He decided to walk to the place. He came to Manukaka's office. It was modest one but well done. He could not find anything gaudy or exaggerated but at the same time nothing was ordinary. The place had warmth reflected when you meet him. When Vishal entered and greeted him, Manukaka was on his cell phone and talking to the person on other end softly and explaining certain procedures of transaction. Vishal understood that the person on the cell was some customer of Manukaka and needed some explanation about some technical legal points of the agreement.

Manukaka indicated Vishal to sit with his free hand. After about 10 minutes, Vishal was receiving the same warm smile followed by same feeling he had experience with Manukaka earlier.

Manukaka said finally after looking at Vishal for few moments lovingly, so you have come finally. I was waiting for you for long time.

Vishal coming out of his daze said to Manukaka, what is happening to me and what is all this?

Manukaka said, nothing, it is just that you were looking for somebody and that person you see in me.

But how could you know? Vishal asked.
Vishalbhai, I could make out from your eyes. They are searching for somebody who would guide you. The eyes are the mirror to your heart.
But how you could recognize it and not others?
That depends on person to person. All here are searching for 'how much could you part with me and how much do I gained from you?' Everybody is looking for easy profits from everyone except few ones.
Vishal said, please guide me Manukaka. I would go mad if not helped.
Aarey... Vishal do not worry, it is not as bad as you think. If one is very sensitive in this field, he would be affected deeply just like you. But it would fade away gradually. Do not worry Vishal you will be alright. Is it alright if I call you Vishal?
Of course, please call me by name. It sounds good. You too had gone through this phase early in your life? asked Vishal eagerly.
Yes Vishal, but nobody to guide me. I learned on my own but I used to talk to one old fellow, a shop owner in this locality from my village. We used to talk for long time. Vishal just stick to your work with full faith and offer services without any expectations. Services to customer is as good as serving God. Just do not hesitate to offer more to them. They may not recognize the value that time but will remember you for long time. And they would refer you customers after customers, which would be enough not only for your survival but prosperity. I have earned multiple times than what you think. I could have retire long back but I like this sector and happiest serving the customers looking for property. It gives me immense pleasure.
But what about most of the people in the sector? asked Vishal
Ah.... the bothering question of Vishalbhai, huh...? said Manukaka mocking & then laughing out loudly.
He continued, when you are dealing with any player in this sector, do not try to judge him. Just accept him the way he is.

That is the first step. This would take some time may be years, but you will get it. Remember just to accept the person and not judging or improving him. With every deal you would start dealing with them in detached fashion and slowly you would start taking the deals in your stride and desired way. Always remember to deal for your customers first. You are here to serve them. If you think you are here to earn only money then you would not last for long time or you would turn like Pradeepbhai always fighting with conscience, getting stressed and spoiling your reputation. If you lose money so be it, just do not be bothered. It will come to you if your intentions are right. I have earned money from unexpected people and with good faith. They still remember me for the generous effort taken by me. So do not bothered about money, it is incidental.

Vishal was listening with full attention and focus. He was overwhelmed with this teachings and his new found guru. He had the same feeling as he had met Manukaka the first time, but this time it was with full force & strength.

After few blank moments he saw Manukaka by his side cajoling his head and saying,

it is alright Vishal, alright, alright…..sshh…sshh…

Vishal asked, what just happened to me?

You fainted.

What are you saying Manukaka?

I think you were overwhelmed by happiness. You were smiling and extremely relaxed when you fainted, said Manukaka smiling affectionately at Vishal.

Vishal instinctively touched Manukaka's feet but Manukaka took Vishal in his arms.

There are few pearls in this turbulent oceans of real estate to be discovered.

But are you the 'deep-diver' in search?

Short Story 8

Property Brokers, know your way!

Neeraj, a property consultant for two years was torn between his emotional turmoil. He was in his office after having an argument with his parents; main reason being not contributing anything to the household expenses. He was facing severe financial crunch affecting his daily routine. He had to pay few pending amounts of bill, EMIs and other biz expenses. He had no work for long time now, except for two small rental deals in the space of 3 months. That was not sufficient for him to sustain. His father was a small businessman staying in a modest home with modest earnings. Neeraj had started real estate brokerage business against his father's wishes.
This situation was faced by lot of other property brokers. They were always treading the line of break-even at the beginning. The few who would digest these situations; establish themselves as real estate brokers and others, would leave the professions blaming the system being unorganized. Neeraj was hard nut and had the experience of facing struggles from the childhood along with the family. Somehow he had begun to believe that real estate would be his forte and would give him immense satisfaction mentally and financially. He was searching for the way desperately to establish himself. He could not fathom the ways of real estate sector for the first 6 months but slowly had come to terms with it and getting comfortable, but at the cost of financial and emotional turmoil which he was facing now. He knew he had to overcome this sooner or later as he would have these moments very often. He was in this deep thought when Sharadbhai, a broker from the neighbouring locality came to his modest office sharing a warm smile. Sharadbhai was a decent fellow with good brokerage practice for last 10 years. He was known for his shrewd biz practices and not letting anybody go off with his brokerage fees. His sweet tone and

language camouflage his sharp biz acumen. It was a sort of a record, where it was believed that the Sharadbhai has lost his brokerage only once in these last 10 years that too because the person owing him had met with fatal accident.
Sharadbhai was saying, how are you Neerajbhai?
Neeraj replied, Sharadbhai I am fine. Thank you, how about you, sir?
Hu to majama choo! Kya hua apne lead ka Neerajbhai?
Mr. Shah (lead/tenant) will come in the evening at 6 pm directly from his office, Neeraj answered spontaneously.
Ok, good. So should I call Pandeyji (Owner) in the evening at your office or my office? asked Sharadbhai.
I think my office as Mr. Shah knows my office or I could get him to your office by 6.30 pm, is that ok? asked Neeraj.
Ok, Neerajbhai, Sharadbhai said & continued after a pause, 'something bothering you?'
How did you know Sharadbhai?
Aarey it is so evident. You are preoccupied, na?
Ha Sharadbhai. Worried about the biz not picking up as I thought.
Aarey... ye to chalta rehta hai... do not worry, everything will be alright in some time. Let time pass by, Sharadbhai said assuring Neeraj.
But Sharadbhai this is the situation every time. I am in two minds with this biz, said Neeraj.
Don't do that Neerajbhai. Real estate need people like you who are intelligent, trustful and professionals. Otherwise anybody becomes real estate agent & spoils the reputation. Yes, sometimes it takes time to establish but that is not because of the market alone.
Meaning? asked Neeraj.
See Neerajbhai, real estate is not a defined field like others. It has lot of ambiguity in it but because of this nature it also has got lot of potential to grow. Real estate is very vast and you have a choice to choose from its various branch.
I am not fully understanding, Sharadbhai! said Neeraj.

Ok, I think you should meet Umeshbhai. He would be a better person. I will call him right now. Are you free now? asked Sharadbhai.

Yes, of-course! Neeraj replied.

After some time Sharadbhai, Neeraj and Umeshbhai were sitting in Umeshbhai's office.

Neeraj had met Umeshbhai few times during the association meetings and other deals but not aware of his background so much. He only knew that he is as senior as Sharadbhai but very shy and conservative in his approach. His low profile status often lead to misjudge his calibre by lots of people, even the realtors. He was an astute realtor with solid integrity and ethical real estate practices. Only few people knew he was one of the most successful realtor and a crorepati multiple times. He knew builders and developers closely but never took & gave undue advantage. Lot of builders and real estate people called him to resolve their private as well as business problems.

This all was explained to Neeraj by Sharadbhai before meeting Umeshbhai.

Sharadbhai said, Once Umeshbhai told me that Neeraj is a very good fellow, so I am taking you to him with your dilemma.

Neeraj was absorbing the importance of this meeting and by the time they reached Umeshbhai's office he was completely nervous.

Sharadbhai explained the purpose of their visit whilst Umeshbhai was listening attentively with occasional smile, nod and 'huhs' in-between. After Sharadbhai finished, Umeshbhai recline back and gave a warm smile towards Neeraj which made him relaxed.

Umeshbhai in his soft but firm voice said, Sharadbhai is right. We need people like you in this field.

Neerajbhai, you may be averse to the field right now because of its irregular income but given a chance and little sense it could give you tremendous returns. This has been my

experience, though I am not as successful, said Umeshbhai modestly and with 'matter-of-fact' tone.
But you are so much successful according to Sharadbhai, said Neeraj.
That is Sharadbhai's greatness to say so!
Neeraj was thinking, if he feels this is not success then what according to him is success?
Neeraj hesistantly asked, would you teach me?
Neerajbhai, you already know so many things and what you need is little push. That we and Sharadbhai would definitely provide you. So do not worry, said Umeshbhai looking at Sandeepbhai who was nodding.
Neeraj said, I have been lucky to meet you 'all, otherwise I was thinking of some extreme measures.
No, no, no… do not even think of it, Neerajbhai. We would extend all the support we could.
Sharadbhai said, you can ask us anything you want to ask.
Neeraj took a long breath and said, I have this dilemma of taking the lead or not. I don't like taking indirect leads as I am not sure of the lead's requirement because when they come to you indirectly they are presented in a very different way. Since we do not understand the need of the prospect first hand you lose the lead and time as well. And when you take initiative to serve such prospects the mediator thinks otherwise about you. So you tend to give up the case. And the second thing is you do not want leave this leads because you are in constant need of money in this biz (though it may not be valid for you both).
Umeshbhai and Sharadbhai were giving a knowing look to Neeraj with a smile.
After deliberate pause, Sharadbhai looked at Umeshbhai giving over the baton.
Umeshbhai looked at Sharadbhai first and then at Neeraj directly into his eyes warmly.
He said, Neerajbhai, you are asking too many questions in one question as it has different perspectives to it. So let us go

one by one. Everybody likes direct leads and serve them without anybody's interference but in real estate there is no regulation for prospects or customers to stick to one fellow realtor, right?

Right, said Neeraj. So he may go to person who charges him less brokerage.

No, this is the false impression everybody has because it is not customer's perspective primarily though he may give you that reason to leave you or to choose cheaper options among the services available in the market.

Meaning? asked Neeraj.

Meaning that the perception of charging lesser brokerage is not right. It is the attitude you present as service provider to customer that decides whether he would go with you or no. Neerajbhai imagine yourself in their shoes and think. Will you not go with person who is caring, understanding and professional in their approach even if you need to pay more.

Yes, if the value given is worth it, replied Neeraj.

Exactly... that is what they are looking for... 'Value' and not price per se. It is our belief that they will not pay. But how do you serve them their worth is the right question?

'By giving excellent service', prompt came the reply from Neeraj.

There you are, Neerajbhai, said Umeshhai.

Umeshbhai continued, People complaining about receiving lesser fees is primarily because they have not served as expected by customers.

And how do you know that you have not served them as expected? asked Neeraj

By simply asking them. Do we do that? no... how do you know it? Ask them why are they paying less and you may find answers for your improvement. Neerajbhai, most of the customers are right most of the time from their point of view, right?

Right, from their view, but our views? asked Neeraj.

Who is paying you? the customer right? then serve him good na... They would not ditch your fees unnecessarily and if they do pay less even after good service they would not badmouth in the market. In fact they would send references. If you have established yourself then you may go in for mandate but for that you need to have niche or USP in the market.

Umeshbhai continued, So as far as possible you avoid indirect cases. And even if you have to serve them, serve them with your 100% effort irrespective of the third party. But how do you get direct cases especially when you are not serving indirect leads (for money) is your second question, right?

Neeraj was nodding with all attention now.

Neerajbhai, for that you have to know your target audience or your ability to attract your customers.

I do not understand, said Neeraj to Umeshbhai intently.

See, you are doing or not doing certain things which is attracting or not attracting customers towards yourself. That is, you are not positioning yourself in the market properly. Somewhere you are not able to attract the customers you would like to come. So you need to find that first.

'So how do I find that?' asked Neeraj.

Ahaa...ha that is the million dollar question, isn't it so? asked Umeshbhai.

This time Neeraj was embarrassed by this as he knew he was asking the most important question in real estate so easily and shamelessly.

Nevertheless, the answer lies within you, continued Umeshbhai.

Howcome Umeshbhai?

Neeraj, you would attract people whom you like or who likes you, right?

Riiii...ght.

Umeshbhai said, Over a period of time (may be 5 years or more) you would attract these people gradually. But this would take long time and even cost you your business or

leaving the biz altogether as is the case now with you. So how do you attract these people in shorter time?
Yesssss? Neeraj understanding the flow.
You have to know yourself first or understand whom you can serve with ease or without any extra effort. This would refine your search a bit. Then understand whether you are in the right locality or place where you find these prospects.
If not then? Asked Neeraj curiously.
Change the locality to your kind of customers. But this is only for initial phase and then slowly it would dawn on you that you could serve anybody and anywhere. But for the initial phase you need to serve in the locality or those prospects where you are comfortable serving.
Why so, Umeshbhai?
See, Neeraj, when you are young and inexperienced you feel stress or uncomfortable serving unknown people because you are always in the fear of losing them; but with slightly known or likeable people you are confident. Hence you may serve to the fullest potential. So as you grow in experience, knowledge and age you get confident and start understanding people correctly and that is when you would serve anybody and anywhere.
But where do you get these prospects, Umeshbhai?
Everywhere, you have to look for it.
I am not understanding.
See for example your case; you being young would understand the issues of young people and couple and hence easy to serve their needs, right?
Right.
But young people may not have money to buy property, right?
Right!
But they could afford property on rent and your locality is the right locality for them as it fits their budgets. You are not concentrating on these people as you should. Just imagine the number of deals you have done in last say 1 year.
I just did rental deals and not a single outright one.

See, now you know that your target should be these customers. So concentrate on these people to begin with and you may be expert in serving them or in another way you are positioning yourself as "rental residential property consultant". These way you would attract customers. So if anybody, even other fellow realtor, needs rental residential properties they know whom to approach. Later you may start expanding accordingly.

I never thought of it in such a way! exclaimed Neeraj.

That is why, I got you to Umeshbhai, said Sandeepbhai after long time.

I am grateful to you both for offering me such advice. Thank you Sandeepbhai & Umeshbhai.

Sandeepbhai said, I told you we do not want to lose you. We are thankful as we would have lost a good realtor and this field needs it desperately.

Umeshbhai was nodding in appreciation.

Short Story 9

The Indian REALTOR

Anyone who is closely associated with real estate is a realtor; but today i am mentioning w.r.t real estate agent, broker or consultant. This is the character who is taken for granted and loathed by many customers. He is never given any credit and is the first casualty in any deal. But why is he so downgraded? Why his image is not appreciated in the society especially in India? The reasons sprinkled are; he is looking for easy money, an opportunist, always looking for soft preys and many more.

Who is responsible for this image? To understand this we need to delve in the history or specifically on the chronology of real estate. To begin with let us consider British rule.

British Colonial influence
British ruled us for almost 150 years. There is bound to be major influence of their way of functioning in our life; in fact our entire constitution till today is the evolved product of their laws. We have to admit though grudgingly, that they were and are better administrator. Our today's administrative field is gift from them. So if any one wants to know how our real estate would evolve further, know the British law. In fact one of the senior lawyer had pointed this fact to me. He also stressed that the 'English' language is a huge factor of our legal system because of its interpretation.

Before British arrived, we were ruled by kings, mughals and other provincial heirs who owned lands (read real estate). After that we were subjected to economic turmoil and subsequently led to growth of zamindars, peshwas and ultimately to English merchants (East India Company). Their presence slowly changed the dynamics of our market and made it more economic dominant (read 'Aarthik'). So merchants or rather traders became more powerful than rulers and reduced them to namesake, so as to say. After the British established themselves with strong and powerful administrative tool there was no way we could change it (still not able to change). This has been passed on as the Indian Registration Act 1908 which is still prevalent and influential in the form of Land Revenue System (Law of the Land). Though registration process as such is /was organised the real estate dealings were not, and any person especially the traders were seen dominating the scene as real estate had an edge over economy (still has). This may have led to exploitation or non-uniform growth in the country where rich people were owning huge stakes of real estate.

Difference between real estate agents, brokers and consultants

In India relations forms a major factor and referring known / unknown person to other known / unknown person for business (read 'dhanda') is huge advantage. This influenced the people in general and led to opportunity of dealing in real estate by any non-professional person making them earn easily or by 'just referring'. These has led to formation of **real estate agents** and is still prevalent in the form of paanwala, chaiwala, security, part time or full time agent with no in-depth knowledge of the sector. They comprise huge percentage in India. But the person doing this as full time with a place or making the parties meet becomes the **'real estate broker'** who facilitates and closes the deal. He is the major player and forms the 'just professional' tag of real estate. He is the person where real estate agents or other players refers the prospective parties. You may have more than one real agent or/and broker in single property deal (some times 15 or more in land deals). As there is no government recognized institute to learn real estate field, we see non-professionals in India. The true professionals have learned the field through experience, knowledge and practicing it and are known as **'real estate consultants'**. These are very few in India and has in-depth knowledge and hunger for the field. Real estate consultants are the professionals were all your real estate issues would be resolved as they are connected with real estate experts of different aspects like legal, taxation, architecture, engineering and others. In today's world where real estate is reaching to the last strata of society, the factors influencing the field is shifted from dealers to end-users as in other fields.

RERA influence
But because of few non-professionals you cannot blame the entire sect. But why does the sector not improve? The answer would be the real estate sector is /was unorganized and allowed all kinds of players; serious as well as non-serious. The bad lot belongs to the non-serious type and as there is no regulation, these kinds were increasing leading to impartial services to property prospects. To protect the end-users (customers) of real estate, government has come with a powerful weapon called 'RERA'. It is the inflection point in real estate as it has lead the foundation for customer centric approach. If the reading on the wall is not read by realtors then they have to pay a huge price for it. RERA and other concrete majors by government is cleaning up the sector and you see professionals entering it or professionalizing the non-professionals. In fact you would see realtors becoming and making efforts to be **real estate consultants**.

There are few real estate organization making sincere effort to organize the field in the form of full /part time courses and government should give them recognition or develop syllabus holistically with them. With RERA the intention is right and process begun.

About Author

Venky (name changed) is in this field for more than a decade with professional background for almost 15 years.
Entrepreneur at heart, is always at new challenges and when introduced to the field of real estate by a legend, as collateral subject to investment was gripped by the field. There was no looking back for him and the journey of understanding & exploring lead to enormous turmoil in his personal & family life. This book was written in one of the lean phases of entrepreneurial journey supported by his wife and two daughters. More than the trouble it was the urge to express the experience with other struggling entrepreneurs which lead to this book.

Copyright@2018 Vinayak N Hanchate

All rights reserved

ISBN – 13: 978-1-9810-7902-5

Indian real estate stories

www.ingramcontent.com/pod-product-compliance
Lightning Source LLC
Chambersburg PA
CBHW031414210526
45464CB00005B/1880